MOON METRO

CONTENTS

PARIS

HOW TO USE THIS BOOK

MAP SECTION

- We've divided Paris into nine distinct areas. Each area has been assigned a color, used on the map itself and in easy-to-spot map number indicators throughout the listings.

- The maps show the location of every listing in the book, using the icon that indicates what type of listing it is (sight, restaurant, etc.) and the listing's locator number.

- The coordinates (in color) indicate the specific grid that the listing is located in. The black number is the listing's locator number. The page number directs you to the listing's full description.

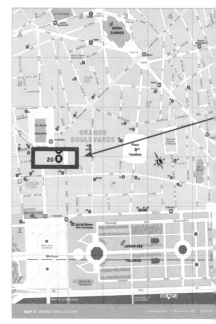

LISTINGS SECTION

- Listings are organized into six sections:

  ⊛ SIGHTS

  ℞ RESTAURANTS

  ℕ NIGHTLIFE

  ⓢ SHOPS

  Ⓐ ARTS AND LEISURE

  ⓗ HOTELS

- Within each section, listings are organized by which map they are located in, then in alphabetical order.

MAP **5** GRANDS BOULEVARDS

LES AMBASSADEURS BUSINESS • FRENCH $$$
Its crystal chandeliers, marble, and mirrors make Les Ambassadeurs as grandly opulent as the fine hotel in which it resides. Politicians and movie moguls enjoy impeccable service and exemplary dishes, such as smoked salmon with whipped cream and caviar and the specialty chocolate tart.
5 **37** HÔTEL DE CRILLON, 10 PL. DE LA CONCORDE, 8E
01-44-71-16-16

ANGELINA CAFÉ • TEA $
This tearoom is almost a century old, and so are some of its customers. The select teas come served in bone china, but the hot chocolate, made with top-quality molten chocolate, is the specialty.
5 **41** 226 RUE DE RIVOLI, 1ER
01-42-60-82-00

ANGL'OPÉRA HOT SPOT • CONTEMPORARY FRENCH $$$
Deconstruction is de rigueur at this upbeat restaurant where the menu is laced with entrées bearing such descriptions as broth of herbs, ginger, soft egg, and foie gras, or roasted Touquet potatoes with sweet garlic, Thai coriander, and beef. But it all comes together to delicious effect.
5 **8** 39 AV. DE L'OPÉRA, 2E
01-42-61-86-25 WWW.EDOUARDHOTEL.COM

AUX LYONNAIS HOT SPOT • LYONNAIS $$
The hype was huge – superchef Alain Ducasse buys tiny bistro to preserve authentic Lyonnais cuisine - but, frankly, deserved. This early-20th-century bistro is charming, from its delightful wall ceramics, zinc bar, and homemade terrines to its excellent service and reasonable prices. It's a must.
5 **3** 32 RUE ST-MARC, 2E
01-42-96-65-04 WWW.ALAIN-DUCASSE.COM

LES BACCHANTES AFTER HOURS • WINE BAR $$
As the name suggests, wine is the only beverage on the menu here. It's not hard to imagine the boisterous mood in this temple to good living, where the food ranges from basic salads and charcuterie to entrecôte and pork.
5 **5** 21 RUE DE CAUMARTIN, 9E
01-42-65-25-35

LE CARRÉ DES FEUILLANTS BUSINESS • FRENCH $$$
Business worthies come here to impress and be impressed. Chef Alain Dutournier demonstrates his mastery of haute cuisine without losing his southwest France origins in such simple-sounding yet sublime dishes as wild hare with truffles and roast chicken with mushrooms.
5 **32** 14 RUE DE CASTIGLIONE, 1ER
01-42-86-82-82

28 MOON METRO

⟵ ⟶ TWO WAYS TO NAVIGATE

1. Scan the map to see what listings are in the area you want to explore. Use the directory to find out the name and page number for each listing.

2. Read the listings to find the specific place you want to visit. Use the map information at the bottom of each listing to find the listing's exact location.

MAP KEY

Major Sights	★
Metro Stop	Ⓜ Ⓡ
Shopping District	⎯⎯⎯
Stairs	�𝐼𝐼𝐼𝐼𝐼𝐼𝐼𝐼
Pedestrian Street	⎯⎯⎯
Arrondissement	▪▪▪▪▪▪▪
Adjacent Map Boundaries	SEE MAP 1

SECTION ICONS

- ⊛ SIGHTS
- Ⓡ RESTAURANTS
- Ⓝ NIGHTLIFE
- Ⓢ SHOPS
- Ⓐ ARTS AND LEISURE
- Ⓗ HOTELS

RESTAURANTS

LES BACCHANTES   DROUANT

IL CORTILE *ROMANTIC • ITALIAN/FRENCH* $$$
In summer, Il Cortile's courtyard, complete with fountain and murals, transports you to Italy, while its food is a superb blend of Italian and French cuisine. Pasta in squid ink and strawberry soup for dessert bring in hotel residents and in-the-know locals. Be sure to book ahead.

MAP 5 C2 Ⓡ 20   HÔTEL CASTILLE, 37 RUE CAMBON, 1ER
01-44-58-45-67

Use the **MAP NUMBER, COLOR GRID COORDINATES,** and **BLACK LOCATOR NUMBER** to find the exact location of every listing in the book.

INTRODUCTION TO
PARIS

For centuries Paris has been known as the City of Light, the City of Romance, and even the Most Beautiful City in the World. And, as many visitors to this popular tourist destination would probably agree, the nicknames endure simply because they're true. But no phrase could ever adequately describe complex character and dramatic extremes of a city that combines sophistication and relaxation, delicacy and debauchery, chic neighborhoods and bawdy boutiques, royal promenades and frenzied shopping streets, ultramodern museums and flamboyantly Gothic cathedrals.

In this dense, congested home to two million, the high cost of living, traffic snarls, and infamous bureaucracy can wear down even the hardiest local. The legendary grumpiness of Parisian waiters can sometimes even seem merited. Still, Paris's allure remains. In fact, its imperfections reveal Paris as a profoundly down-to-earth place despite its larger-than-life reputation. Couples kiss on park benches while blue-haired grandmothers feed pigeons. People meet on the steps of the Opéra Garnier and sunbathe at the foot of the Tour Eiffel. An appreciation for the little pleasures of life takes precedence.

Paris is famous the world over for the love of good food enjoyed at leisure, the primacy of fashion and people-watching, and the strict social graces that structure daily life. Despite inroads by fast food, Parisians still prefer to spend their Sunday mornings at the mar-

MULTICULTURAL PARIS

Cosmopolitan in every sense of the word, Parisians not only come from all corners of the "hexagon" (as France is affectionately called), but from every corner of the globe. Immigration in the early 20th century was mainly from other European countries, particularly Portugal, Spain, and Italy. But ever since the 1960s, citizens from distant territories and former French colonies have made Paris their new home. The multicultural Belleville district is home to people from Algeria, Morocco, Tunisia, French Polynesia, the Caribbean, China, Vietnam, and Cambodia. Within this vibrant jumble of faces, fashions, and accents lives the old adage that being Parisian is less about where you're born than having the right attitude – that certain je ne sais quoi.

ket jockeying for the best roasted chicken or stinkiest Camembert.

The same zest inspires style mavens, forever cultivating Le Look – a person's total style that's more about knowing what's flattering than what's trendy. The urban crunch that serves the fashion-forward also makes the rules of propriety and courtesy critically important to all Parisians. These little gestures act both as a nod to the past and a social password. Every conversation should begin with *"bonjour,"* whether you're buying bread or an Hermès scarf. And everyone has the right to be addressed as Monsieur or Madame. Do as the Parisians do, and you'll receive the same courtesy in return.

With this combination of imperial grandeur and local air, Paris owes its sheer beauty not only to its material charm, but also to its approach to a civilized and refined way of life. It's no wonder that the city has been adopted over the centuries by so many artists and thinkers – and continues to hold an idealized place in many a traveler's imagination.

HISTORY

This grand city started off as a settlement of a Gallic fishing tribe known as the Parisii on an island in the Seine River. During the Roman Empire, it became an important city called Lutetia (or Lutèce, in French) – vestiges from the Roman era can still be found on the Left Bank.

GETTING AROUND

Paris's efficient public transportation system is one of the best in the world. An intricate system of buses, 14 Métro lines, five regional RER trains, and three trams make it a cinch to get around town without the burden of a rental car. And anyone with a weekly transportation pass gets a discount on Batobus river bus tickets. Even with the unfortunate frequency of personnel strikes, minimal service is always guaranteed. Its only *point noir,* regularly called into question by Parisians tired of running for the last Métro at 12:45 A.M. like urban Cinderellas, is the lack of 24-hour service. Finding a taxi at 2 A.M. on a Saturday night requires patience, especially if it's raining. As a last resort, night owls can try cramming aboard one of the few Noctambus buses that circulate hourly between 1 A.M. and 5 A.M.

Although the availability of public transit eases the stress of getting from place to place, be sure to take some time to walk around. Paris is also a surprisingly compact city best seen on foot. You can often walk from one museum to another, past manicured parks, colonnaded courtyards, chic boutiques, and buzzing cafés, and get a taste of Parisian life at street level.

After the fall of the Holy Roman Empire and subsequent invasions by barbarian tribes, Paris discovered Christianity. Clovis became its first Catholic king in A.D. 500, establishing the city as the capital of the slowly expanding French kingdom. Despite Europe's wars and plagues, Paris prospered throughout the medieval and Renaissance eras. With the Age of Enlightenment, Parisians rebelled against the supremacy of the clergy and nobility, resulting in the French Revolution of 1789 and the end of the French monarchy.

A chaotic procession of democratic presidents, constitutional monarchs, and two ambitious emperors marked the 19th century. The first emperor, Napoléon Bonaparte, crowned himself in 1804 and embarked on an ambitious military campaign that would result in his 1815 abdication and exile. Bonaparte's nephew followed suit as Napoléon III in 1850 and is credited with transforming Paris into a modern city by annexing villages such as Montmartre and tearing through the old medieval streets with tree-lined boulevards and parks.

The 1870 Franco-Prussian war brought an end to his rule, and after a bloody civil conflict known as the Commune, Paris settled on its current system of democratic republicanism.

The 20th century began with the 1900 World's Fair construction of belle epoque monuments such as the Tour Eiffel, Grand Palais, and Gare d'Orsay. After the casualties of the Great War and the Nazi occupation during World War II, Paris took a while to recover: It wouldn't be until the 1970s that it would finally take on the challenges of modernizing the city while preserving its historic architectural treasures.

CULTURE ON THE CHEAP

Paris's commitment to culture is evident in the accessibility of its treasures. This means that if you've got champagne tastes and a beer budget, Paris won't disappoint. In fact, most of the city's cultural sights can be enjoyed without spending one euro. The permanent collections of all 15 municipal museums are free to the public (including the Musée Carnavalet and Musée de la Vie Romantique), and national museums such as the Louvre and Musée d'Orsay are free every first Sunday of the month. Parc de la Villette hosts free open-air cinema in late summer, and Parc Floral in the Bois de Vincennes hosts free jazz and classical music concerts on weekend afternoons summer-fall. The most impressive freebie is undoubtedly Paris Plage, started in 2001 by Mayor Delanoë to turn the roads along the Seine into an urban beach complete with palm trees, chaise longes, and sand volleyball during the summer months.

NOTRE-DAME   TOUR EIFFEL   SACRÉ-COEUR BASILICA

THE BEST OF
PARIS

Paris offers so many amazing sights that it's hard to know where to start. A day in this city can include seeing some of the most famous works of Western art, browsing street markets, and people-watching in manicured gardens. Here is one way to visit some of the city's many monuments, and get a taste of the way the locals live while you're at it.

1 There's no better place to start a tour of Paris than the Ile de la Cité, the oldest part of Paris and home to legendary **Notre-Dame (p. 2).** Get a gargoyle's-eye view of Paris from the north tower.

2 Stroll through the colorful **Marché aux Fleurs (p. 50)** at Place Lepine – you'll feel like you're walking through a painting since this flower market has been depicted in many.

3 Your last stop on the island is tiny **Ste-Chapelle (p. 3),** for a look at its kaleidoscope of 50-foot-tall stained-glass windows.

4 Follow the Pont Neuf across the Seine and walk through the St-Germain-des-Prés district en route to the **Musée d'Orsay (p. 8).** Here, you'll find Impressionist and post-Impressionist artworks by Degas, Rodin, and Monet. For lunch, the museum has two cafés and a beautiful belle epoque restaurant.

5 The pedestrian Pont Solferino takes you across the Seine and to the **Jardin des Tuileries (p. 11),** where the many chairs dotted around the formal French gardens make for great people-watching.

6 Head toward the glass pyramid marking the entrance to the **Louvre (p. 12).** It would be impossible to see everything in one quick trip, but its three most famous works – the Mona Lisa, Winged Victory, and Venus de Milo – are conveniently located in the Denon Wing.

7 To recover from all the museum-hopping, take the metro to St-Paul and explore the Marais neighborhood, a maze of medieval-era streets and 17th-century mansions. Window-shop along **rue des Francs Bourgeois (p. 61),** where trendy stores offer jewelry, home furnishings, and gift items.

8 Make your way to the **Tour Eiffel (p. 9),** by metro or taxi, as evening is the best time to see it. Take the elevator to the top floor for panoramic views of Paris.

9 Ride the metro to Montmartre (get off at Abbesses), a neighborhood of pretty stairway streets. For dinner, choose one of the tiny bistros, such as homey **L'Entracte (p. 36).**

10 Finish off the day on the stairs leading up to **Sacré-Coeur Basilica (p. 16).** From these steps you can see all of Paris before you, a sparkling City of Light.

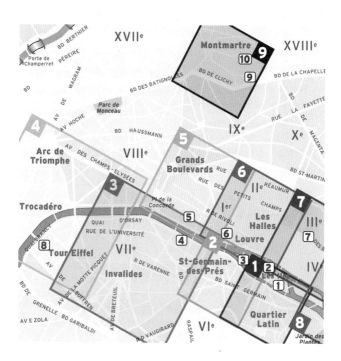

PONT ALEXANDRE III

PARIS
AFTER DARK

The City of Light comes alive after dark. This ambitious tour lets you experience the extraordinary beauty of the city's illuminations as well as the excitement of its vibrant nightlife. Make sure you're well rested – the clubs of Paris stay open until dawn, when you can greet the rising sun with a hot bowl of onion soup.

1 Start off your evening with a happy hour cocktail at one of the city's trendy bars, such as **Le Fumoir (p. 43),** a sleek and sexy bar and restaurant behind the Louvre.

2 Head toward the Seine, crossing at the **Passerelle des Arts (p. 5)** pedestrian bridge. Its views of the Eiffel Tower, Ile de la Cité, and the Grand Palais make it a popular place to watch the sun set over the city.

3 At the end of the bridge, take the steps down to the Quai Malaquais, where you can embark on a peaceful river cruise aboard the **Batobus (p. 81).** Stay on as the boat makes its loop of the islands and glides past the Louvre. Disembark at the Champs-Elysées stop, close to **Pont Alexandre III (p. 8).**

4 Walk to the Invalides area and search out **Le Café Thoumieux (p. 41),** *the* spot in the 7th for a drink in luxurious surrounds.

5 Metro line 6 will take you directly to the Etoile, where the **Arc de Triomphe (p. 9)** stands proudly at the intersection of 12 avenues. From the rooftop platform you'll be able to admire the perfectly aligned Voie Triomphale, a string of illuminated monuments stretching from the Grande Arche de La Défense to the Louvre.

6 After all those stairs, it's time to refuel with a late dinner (Parisians never dine before 8 P.M.) at one of the city's venerable jazz clubs like **Le Bilboquet (p. 40).**

7 Top off your dinner with a shot of strong Parisian espresso at nearby **Café de Flore (p. 22)** to keep you awake for the rest of the night.

8 The city's clubs don't get going until midnight. Warm up at **Cab (p. 43)** − short for Cabaret − a retro-futuristic nightclub popular with fashion and media jet-setters.

9 Then let your hair down at the city's wildest Latin club, **Favela Chic (p. 48).** A tightly packed, mojito-fueled crowd dances on the tables until dawn every weekend.

10 Finish your evening in Parisian style with a bowl of onion soup at the historic 24-hour brasserie **Au Pied de Cochon (p. 30).**

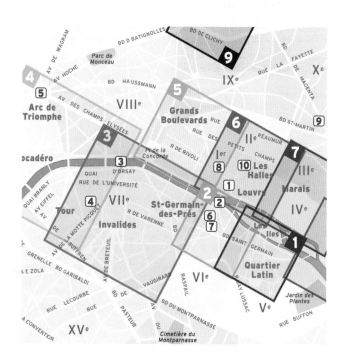

LES DEUX MAGOTS PANTHÉON   JARDIN DES PLANTES

INTELLECTUAL
PARIS

Paris has a long history of attracting artists, writers, and other intellectuals to live in its apartments, work in its studios, and debate in its cafés. The Latin Quarter has been the stomping ground of students since the Middle Ages, and St-Germain-des-Prés has been a favorite among many luminaries. Here's a day where you can explore the haunts and landmarks that show that Paris has both beauty *and* brains.

1 Start with a coffee at **Les Deux Magots (p. 22),** once frequented by Oscar Wilde, Arthur Rimbaud, and Ernest Hemingway.

2 The **Musée National Eugène Delacroix (p. 67)** is nearby. Housed in the artist's former home, the collection of lesser-known works complements those in the Louvre and Musée d'Orsay.

3 Make your way to Quartier de la Huchette just off the busy Place St-Michel. Follow the cobblestone pedestrian streets past the dubious-quality tourist restaurants and crepe stands to the neighborhood's legendary English bookstore, **Shakespeare and Co. (p. 50),** for a copy of Hemingway's *A Moveable Feast* or a translation of Baudelaire's *Paris Spleen*.

4 Head past the Sorbonne University, open since the 13th century, to the neighboring **Panthéon (p. 4),** the Latin Quarter's most prominent monument. The crypt is the resting place of French heroes such as Marie Curie and Alexandre Dumas.

5 Just behind the Panthéon is the historic **rue Mouffetard (p. 4),** one of the city's original routes to Rome. Gather your picnic supplies from the gourmet boutiques and food stalls of this bustling market street.

6 Enjoy your picnic in the 400-year-old **Jardin des Plantes (p. 15),** opened in the early 1600s by the king's doctors as a place to grow medicinal herbs. Its magnificent flowering gardens are also home to the fascinating galleries of the National Museum of Natural History.

7 Nearby, the **Institut du Monde Arabe (p. 66)** will expand your knowledge of Arabic arts and culture. The striking architecture alone justifies a visit.

8 For dinner, make your way to **L'Escargot Montorgueil (p. 30).** Besides specializing in snails, this bistro has a list of patrons that includes Charlie Chaplin and Salvador Dalí.

9 End your day of intellectualizing with a movie at **Le Champo (p. 75).** Near the Sorbonne, this art house theater screens independent films from present-day luminaries.

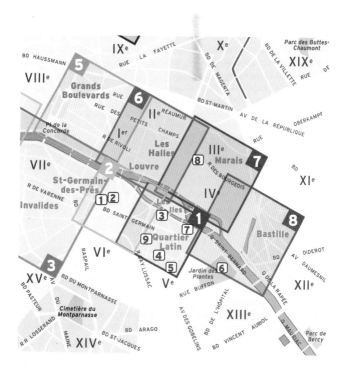

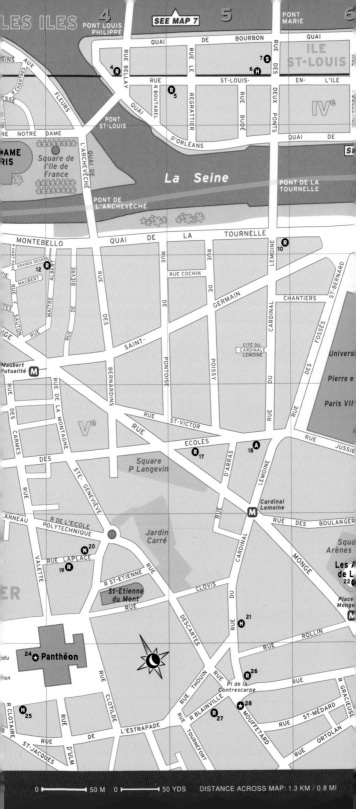

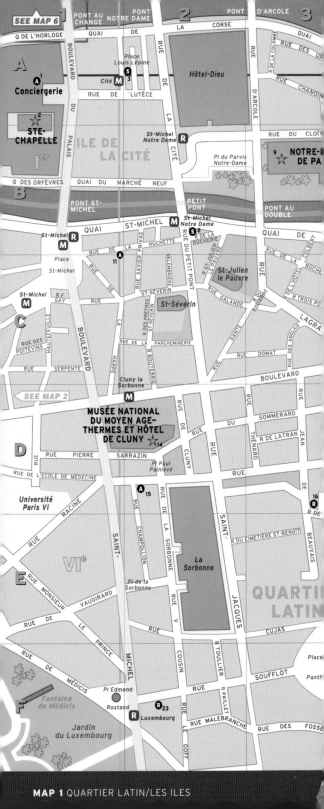

MAP 1 QUARTIER LATIN/LES ILES

QUARTIER LATIN/LES ILES

First developed by the Gallo-Romans, Ile de la Cité and the Latin Quarter are the oldest districts in Paris. During the Middle Ages, French kings built the sights that the island is known for today: Notre-Dame Cathedral, the Conciergerie, and the Palais de la Cité's private Ste-Chapelle. On the Left Bank, monasteries and the Sorbonne attracted students from all over Europe whose only common language was Latin, giving the area its "Latin Quarter" moniker. In the 20th century this student-dominated center of bohemianism and radicalism was the starting point of the May 1968 riots that resulted in a nation-wide workers strike.

Today tourism and fast food have invaded much of the Quartier Latin, particularly around the boulevard St-Michel and rue de la Huchette. But its narrow cobblestone streets are still worth exploring. Major sights include the world-famous Musée de Cluny medieval museum, the Institut du Monde Arabe center for Arabic arts, and the imposing Panthéon, a monument to France's heroes such as Voltaire and Victor Hugo. For shopping, don't miss the rue Mouffetard market street immortalized in Ernest Hemingway's *A Moveable Feast* or the upscale gift boutiques of the adorable Ile St-Louis, the smaller Seine island next to Ile de la Cité.

MAP 1 QUARTIER LATIN/LES ILES

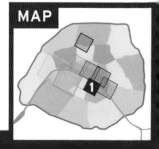

MAP

1

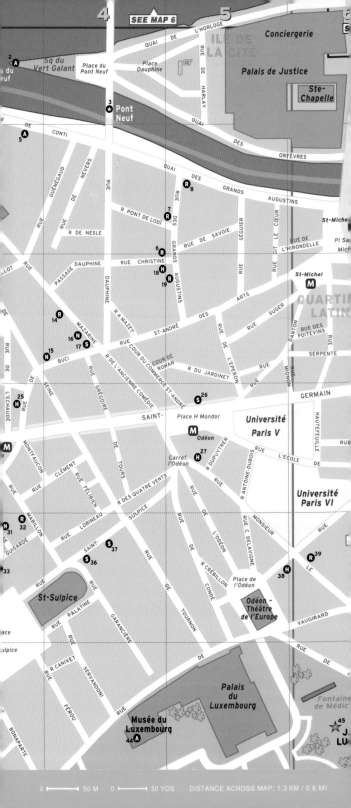

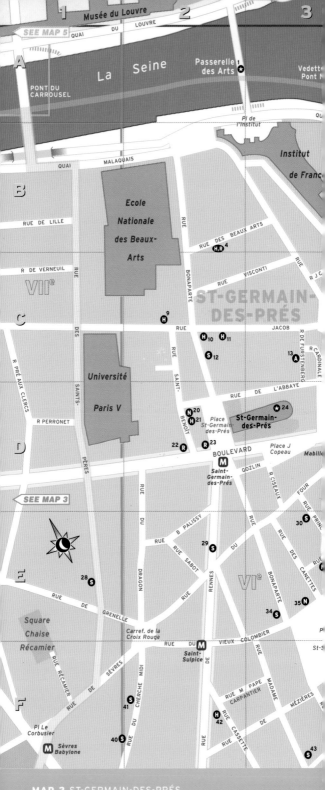

MAP 2 ST-GERMAIN-DES-PRÉS

ST-GERMAIN-DES-PRÉS

The St-Germain-des-Prés district, on the north end of the 6th arrondissement, is named for one of the oldest churches in Paris, which is the only remaining remnant of a vast Benedictine abbey destroyed during the Revolution. From the 1940s to the 1970s, the neighborhood attracted intellectuals, artists, and writers to jazz clubs and famous cafés like Les Deux Magots and Café de Flore.

Since the 1990s, St-Germain-des-Prés has become more upscale, with fashion boutiques replacing bookshops. Art galleries and interior decorating shops line the streets around the Ecole Nationale des Beaux-Arts (School of Fine Arts), while farther east, fruit stalls, gourmet food stores, and sidewalk cafés make rue de Buci perfect for people-watching. But the district is not all retail therapy: Escape the crowds at the romantic Jardin du Luxembourg, a formal French garden of tree-lined gravel alleys, sculpted fountains, and elaborate floral displays.

MAP 2 ST-GERMAIN-DES-PRÉS

MAP

2

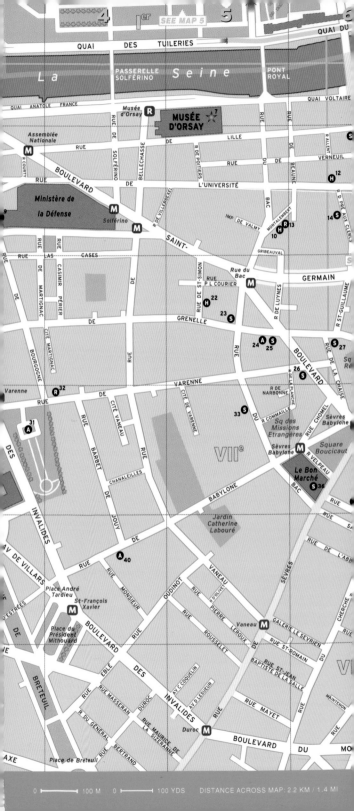

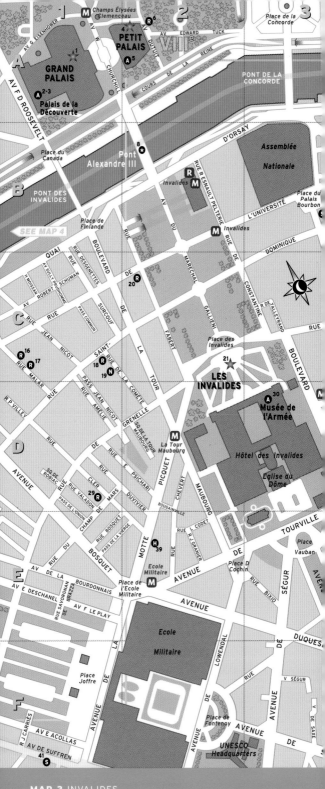

MAP 3 INVALIDES

INVALIDES

The diamond-shaped 7th arrondissement houses the wealthiest part of the Left Bank, where government offices and foreign embassies occupy many opulent town houses. Its wide avenues offer perfectly aligned views of landmarks and refreshing open spaces. Manicured gardens and bronze cannons surround its most imposing monument, the Hôtel des Invalides, built by Louis XIV as a refuge for wounded and retired soldiers. Beneath the golden Eglise du Dôme lies the tomb of Emperor Napoléon I. Next door is the aristocratic Hôtel Biron, an 18th-century mansion housing the Musée Rodin and a romantic sculpture garden.

Overlooking the Seine is the Musée d'Orsay, the former belle epoque train station transformed into the museum for French Impressionist and post-Impressionist arts. The grand complex in the shadow of the Tour Eiffel is the Ecole Militaire, the still-active military academy where Napoléon trained as an officer. On a more human-scale, the charming rue Cler market street brings together a mix of food shops, cafés, and open-air stalls. For high fashion shopping, follow the chic *Parisiennes* to the Bon Marché department store at Sèvres Babylone.

MAP 3 INVALIDES

MAP

3

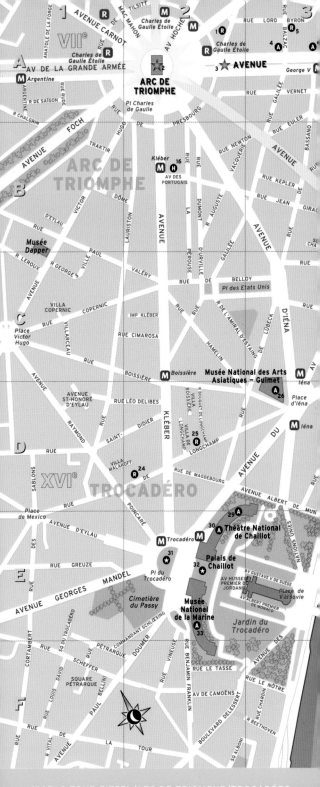

MAP 4 TOUR EIFFEL/ARC DE TRIOMPHE/TROCADÉRO

TOUR EIFFEL/ ARC DE TRIOMPHE/ TROCADÉRO

The western expanse of the capital represents the height of Parisian pomp and glitz. Constructed in the 19th century, Napoleon's magnificent 19th-century military monument, the Arc de Triomphe, stands as a cornerstone of this area. It is the hub of 12 radiating avenues, including the famous Champs-Elysées. This tree-lined avenue of upscale shops and fast food chains, along with avenues George V and Montaigne make up the Golden Triangle, home to top couture houses.

Beyond, the posh 16th arrondissement is a haven for art lovers, with the Musée Guimet of Asian arts, the Palais de Tokyo's contemporary art lab, and the Musée de la Mode's historic fashion collection. The vast esplanade of the neo-classical Palais de Chaillot is the best place to admire the city's most beloved monument, the Tour Eiffel, framed by the shooting water cannons of the Tocadéro Gardens.

MAP 4 TOUR EIFFEL/ARC DE TRIOMPHE/TROCADÉRO

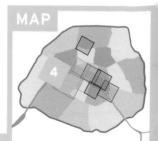

MAP

4

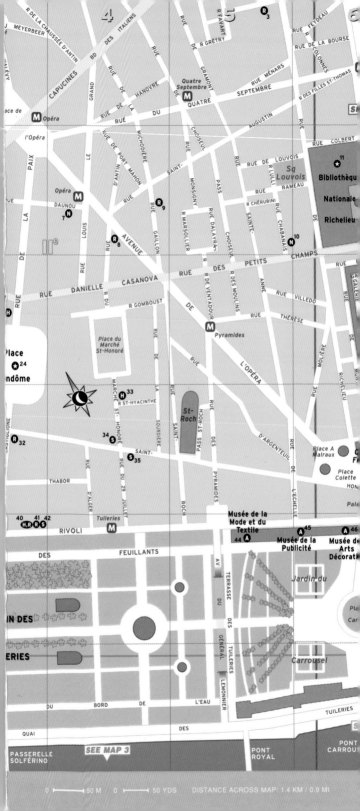

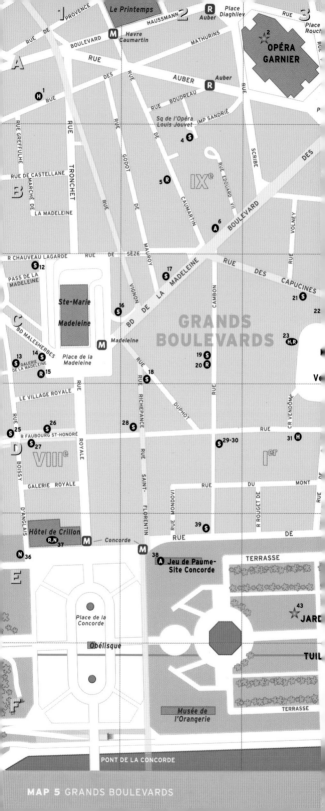

MAP 5 GRANDS BOULEVARDS

GRANDS BOULEVARDS

First created when Louis XIV converted the city's 17th-century fortifications into wide promenades, boulevards really came of age in the 19th century, when they replaced the choked alleys of medieval Paris. Branching out from the Opéra Garnier and the Place de la Madeleine, the Grands Boulevards became the stomping grounds of the fashionable bourgeoisie. Today these roads remain popular among shopaholics undeterred by the constant stream of noisy traffic. Behind Charles Garnier's opera house, on the boulevard Haussmann, are two of the city's grandest department stores, Le Printemps and Galeries Lafayette. Down boulevard de la Madeleine, the Greek temple-turned-church of the same name is surrounded by gourmet shops like Fauchon and Hédiard. Mouths will water at window dressings on the Place Vendôme, land of ritzy jewelers, and along rue St-Honoré, where fashionistas hunt down the latest trends.

Escape commercial temptation at the Jardin des Tuileries, where you can enjoy a bucolic stroll beneath the trees or participate in the ultimate Paris activity: people-watching. The sport can continue into the evening as the brasseries and cafés around the Opéra fill with a lively post-theater crowd.

MAP 5 GRANDS BOULEVARDS

La
Bourse

AP 6

GALERIE COLBERT

JOLAIS
JOLAIS

in

u

alais

Royal

Palais
Royal

Musée
e
M

sée du
ouvre

P 2

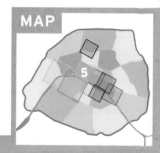

MAP

5

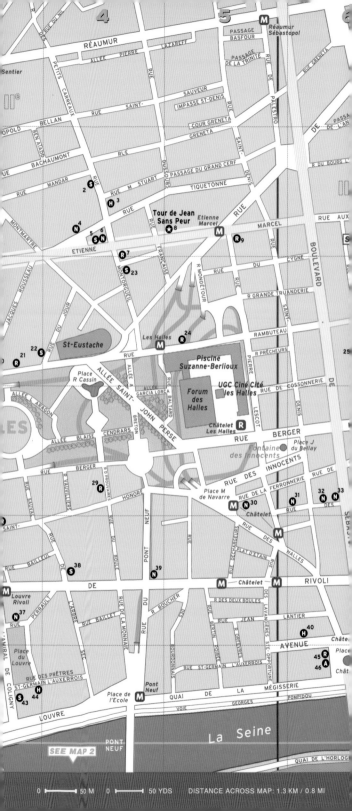

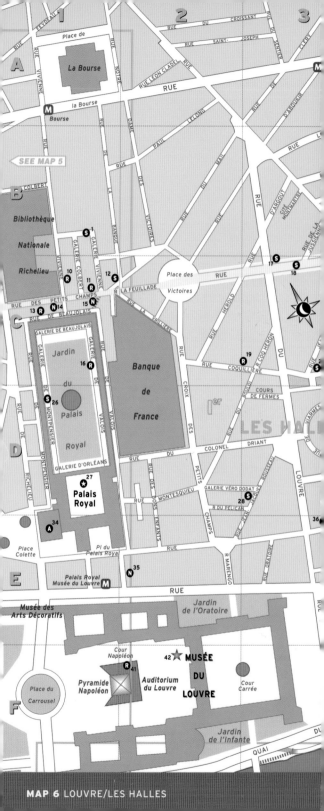

MAP 6 LOUVRE/LES HALLES

LOUVRE/LES HALLES

Located between the Arc de Triomphe/Champs-Elysées pomp and the Marais frenzy, this area balances the frenetic motion of its neighbors with the frozen grandeur of its monuments. The Musée du Louvre beckons visitors from around the world to its grand galleries. Next door, the historic theater of the Comédie Française hides within the gardens and stately arcades of the Palais Royal. Just beyond are 19th-century shopping arcades like the Galerie Vivienne.

But this center is hardly static. Cross the elegant Place des Victoires to the rue Etienne-Marcel for streetwise fashions and trendy cafés. Pedestrian streets surrounding the charming rue Montorgueil have become one of the city's hot new nightspots. However, skip the Forum des Halles shopping mall, an unfortunate 1960s modernist effort surrounded by tacky boutiques, fast-food shops, and a sprinkling of sex shops. Opt instead for a relaxed stroll in the smaller side streets of rue de Rivoli.

MAP 6 LOUVRE/LES HALLES

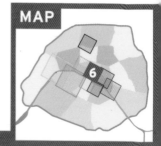

MAP

6

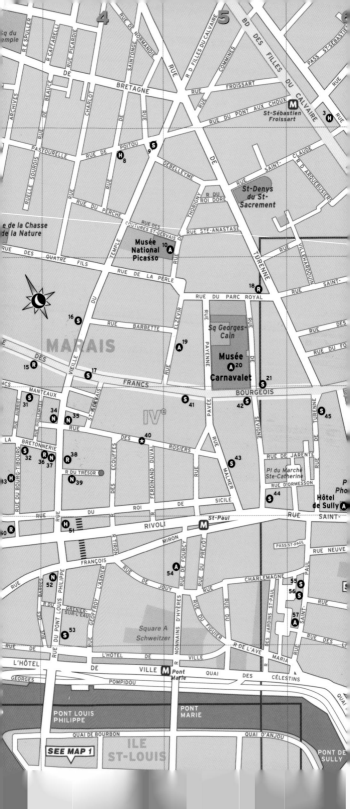

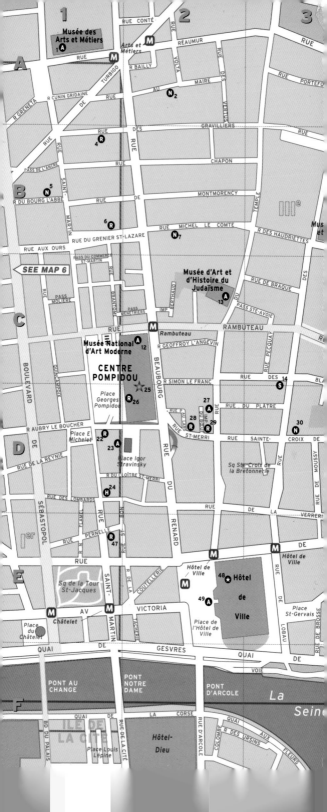

MARAIS

A web of narrow streets bursting with mansions, museums, and secret gardens, the Marais preserves much of the best Renaissance architecture in Paris. Originally a swamp (*marais* is French for marsh), it became the epicenter of French aristocracy in 1605 with the construction of the Place des Vosges. After Louis XIV moved the court to Versailles, the Marais declined and degenerated into a slum. Ambitious restoration work in the late 1960s brought the neighborhood back to its former glory. Many of its mansions, or *hôtel particulier*, have been converted into museums, such as the Musée Picasso and the Musée Carnavalet. Centre Pompidou adds some new architecture to the mix with its bold, striking design.

The Marais is one of Paris's most vibrant neighborhoods. The rue Vielle du Temple is lively night and day, lined with trendy cafés and hip clothing stores. It's also the center of gay and lesbian life in Paris, particularly along the rue Ste-Croix de la Bretonnerie. One part of the Marais that has remained fairly constant through the centuries is the Jewish Quarter, centered on rue des Rosiers. High fashion has encroached upon its synagogues and kosher delis, but the street still feels authentic.

MAP 8 BASTILLE

BASTILLE

Nothing remains of the Bastille prison, stormed by the revolutionary mob on July 14, 1789, but Place de la Bastille still has a revolutionary kick. The modern Opéra Bastille, inaugurated on the 1989 Bastille Day Bicentennial, overlooks the square's Colonne de Juillet, built to commemorate the 1830 revolutionaries and a rallying point for political demonstrations.

Nearby, the rue de Lappe and rue de la Roquette reverberate with student nightlife venues blaring salsa and techno. Just past the faubourg St-Antoine's famous wood-working workshops is the Marché Aligre, one of the liveliest open markets in Paris, and the high-end galleries of the Viaduc des Arts, located under the arcades of the Promenade Plantée's elevated garden trail.

Across the river, the beloved Jardin des Plantes holds, as its name suggests, numerous varieties of plants and trees. Summer is a particularly fun time for this area, when the Square Tino Rossi hosts open-air dancing every night.

MAP 8 BASTILLE

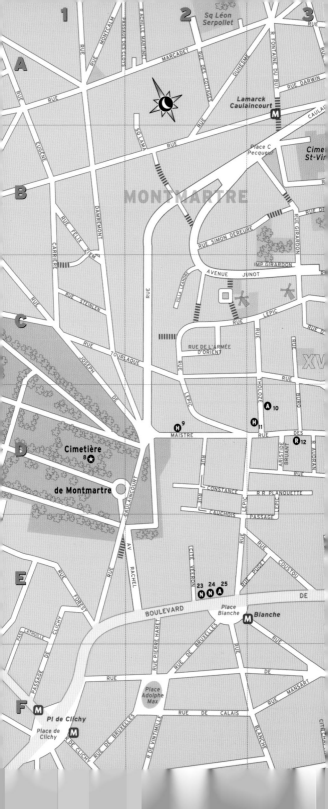

MONTMARTRE

At the turn of the 20th century, Montmartre was home to a thriving community of artists that included Van Gogh and Picasso. Today, aggressive artists in the famed Place du Tertre will compete to sketch your portrait or sell you an "Impressionist" sunset. Although pretty, the chalky white Sacré-Coeur Basilica that dominates the hillside has all the atmosphere of a crowded elevator. But despite the touristy air of the neighborhood's main attractions, the charm remains in its picturesquely steep staircases and quieter streets on the north side of the hill. This is where the grapes ripen in Paris' only remaining vineyard, Le Clos Montmartre, and two ancient windmills still stand on the rue Lepic, not far from the café Les Deux Moulins, made famous in Jean-Pierre Jeunet's hit movie *Amélie*.

On the south side of the hill is the Pigalle district and the historic can-can cabarets that were immortalized by Toulouse-Lautrec. Today it's more seedy than racy – the neon sex shops are slowly being replaced by more legitimate entertainment venues. But the Moulin Rouge endures, offering a Las Vegas–style show and overpriced food.

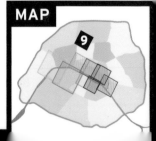

MAP

9

★ SIGHTS

MAP 1 QUARTIER LATIN/LES ILES

MUSÉE NATIONAL DU MOYEN AGE – THERMES ET HÔTEL DE CLUNY

Commonly known as the Musée de Cluny, this museum has one of Europe's finest collections of medieval artifacts, including the famous *Lady and the Unicorn* tapestries and 21 of the original statues from Notre-Dame's facade, knocked off by French revolutionaries and discovered during road construction. The museum has many other precious exhibits, including stained-glass panels from St-Denis and Ste-Chapelle and illuminated books. In 1998 a new section was added, which portrays everyday life at the end of the Middle Ages. Like many museums in Paris, the setting alone – a remarkably well-preserved 15th-century abbey built right up against the remains of a Gallo-Roman-era bathhouse – is worth a visit. In 2000 a neo-medieval public garden was added, with 58 species of the flora depicted in the *Lady and the Unicorn,* including lily of the valley, hawthorn, giant daffodil, and daisy. There are also herbs such as mint, sage, absinthe, and thyme, prized in the Middle Ages for their medicinal qualities.

MAP 1 D2❶14   6 PL. PAUL PAINLEVÉ, 5E 01-53-73-78-00
WWW.MUSEE-MOYENAGE.FR
HOURS: WED.-MON. 9:15 A.M.-5:45 P.M.

NOTRE-DAME DE PARIS

Architects, craftspeople, and artists labored for nearly two centuries (1163-1345) to build Notre-Dame, France's most famous cathedral. On the architectural side, its flying buttresses (best admired from the banks of the Latin Quarter) and stained-glass windows attract the most attention. But Notre-Dame is really famous for its role in French history as one of the city's oldest cathedrals, built on the ruins of a Roman temple and witness to events such as Napoléon crowning himself emperor. Later generations of Parisians altered, plundered, and restored it, from Viollet-le-Duc's addition of the neo-Gothic spire and famous gargoyle statues in the late 1800s to the restoration and cleaning of the cathedral's facade in 2000. There's even a low-voltage shock system to keep pigeons off the gargoyles. Despite the constant traffic of camera-wielding visitors, masses are still performed regularly, including Sunday-afternoon recitals on one of the largest organs in France.

MUSÉE NATIONAL DU MOYEN AGE   NOTRE-DAME DE PARIS   STE-CHAPELLE

To avoid crowds, visit early in the morning. If you want the same view as the gargoyles, climb the 387 steps of the north bell tower, past the 13-ton Emmanuel bell, still hanging from its original supports, and up onto the fenced-in balcony. Underneath Notre-Dame, the Crypte Archéologique holds ancient building foundations and vestiges of Paris's history dating back to Roman times, with scenes of everyday life on the Ile de la Cité from the 3rd through 18th century.

 B3●9 PL. DU PARVIS NOTRE-DAME, 4E 01-42-34-56-10
HOURS: DAILY 8 A.M.-6:45 P.M. (TOWER 9:30 A.M.-7:30 P.M. IN HIGH SEASON)

STE-CHAPELLE

Few sights, even in Paris, rival the royal chapel of Ste-Chapelle. This tiny jewel of Gothic architecture, built in the 13th century 100 years before Notre-Dame, has a series of 16 exquisite stained-glass windows constituting the sides and end of the sanctuary. The windows rise to the vaulted ceiling and are held in place by the frailest possible stonework. Louis IX (a.k.a. St-Louis) commissioned Ste-Chapelle to house the religious relics he bought back from the Crusades, all of which are now in Notre-Dame. Created by nameless master craftspeople, the windows are probably the oldest in Paris. They depict the entire history of creation and redemption – to the medieval mind – in 1,134 different scenes, rendered in infinite shades of sapphire, ruby, emerald, and topaz. A great rose window, added in the 15th century, completes the collection. It contains 86 panes of glass and tells the story of the Apocalypse. Though it looks fragile, the miraculous chapel is solid – no cracks have appeared in the delicate vaulting in seven centuries. Try to visit on a sunny day and bring binoculars. Take a wall seat and read the windows left to right, from bottom to top. There's also a regular schedule of classical music concerts in the chapel throughout the year.

MAP 1 A1○2 BD. DU PALAIS, 1ER 01-53-40-60-80
HOURS: APR.-SEPT. DAILY 9:30 A.M.-6 P.M., OCT.-MAR. DAILY 9 A.M.-5 P.M.

LES ARÈNES DE LUTÈCE
A vestige of Paris's Roman past tucked into the Latin Quarter, the arena was rediscovered during construction in 1869. Once 17,000 people could watch gruesome spectacles here; now children come to play in ancient dust.

MAP 1 E6○22   ACCESS VIA RUE MONGE AND RUE DE NAVARRE, 5E

PANTHÉON
Louis XV's Greek-style church was transformed by the French Revolution into a temple dedicated to the greats of French history such as Voltaire, Victor Hugo, Emile Zola, Pierre and Marie Curie, Alexandre Dumas, and Resistance leader Jean Moulin.

MAP 1 F3○24   PL. DU PANTHÉON, 5E
01-44-32-18-00   WWW.MONUM.FR

RUE MOUFFETARD
One of the oldest market streets in Paris, Mouffetard is lined with cafés, cheap restaurants, clothing shops, gourmet-food boutiques, and market stalls every day but Monday.

MAP 1 F5○28   RUE MOUFFETARD BTWN. PL. DE LA CONTRESCARPE AND RUE CENSIER, 5E

MAP 2 ST-GERMAIN-DES-PRÉS

JARDIN DU LUXEMBOURG
The wildly popular Jardin du Luxembourg (Luxembourg Garden) functions as a green oasis on the bustling Left Bank with 60 acres of formal gardens extending south from the Palais du Luxembourg. A favorite of visitors and residents alike, the gardens are embellished with 100 statues, leafy avenues, and an ornate octagonal pond on which generations of Parisian children have sailed toy boats. The splendid baroque Fontaine de Médicis pays homage to Marie de Médici, who built the Luxembourg gardens and palace after the assassination of her husband Henri II in 1612 to remind her of her native Florence. She never lived in the palace though, after being banished to the countryside for scheming against Richelieu, adviser to her son, King Louis XIII. Since 1804, it has housed the French Senate, except dur-

PANTHÉON   JARDIN DU LUXEMBOURG

ing World War II when the German Luftwaffe made it their headquarters. Next to the Senate, the Musée du Luxembourg hosts prestigious temporary art exhibits, while the garden gates have been used as a perfect outdoor gallery ever since Yann-Arthus Bertrand's majestic "The Earth Seen from the Sky" photos first awed passersby in 2000. Sit in the wrought-iron chairs and watch the strollers, necking couples, old men playing *boules* (akin to lawn bowling), chess players, and daydreamers. There are also children's pony rides, a marionette house, a bandstand, and an open-air café.

 F6 ✪45   RUE DE VAUGIRARD AT RUE DE MÉDICIS, 6E 01-42-34-25-95
(MUSÉE DU LUXEMBOURG)
GARDEN HOURS: APR.-OCT. DAILY 7:30 A.M.-9:30 P.M.,
NOV.-MAR. DAILY 8:15 A.M.-5 P.M.
MUSEUM HOURS: MON., FRI., SAT., SUN. 11 A.M.-10 P.M.,
WED., THURS. 11 A.M.-7 P.M.

EGLISE ST-GERMAIN-DES-PRÉS
This is the oldest church in Paris and most of the surviving architecture is from the 11th and 12th centuries. It's one of the few Parisian churches with a painted interior.

 D3 ✪24   3 PL. ST-GERMAIN-DES-PRÉS, 6E
01-43-25-41-71

PASSERELLE DES ARTS
No bridge has more romantic views of central Paris than the footbridge Passerelle des Arts (Pont des Arts) – the Seine's first metal bridge.

 A2 ✪1   ENTER AT QUAI DE CONTI AND PL. DE L'INSTITUT, 1ER

PONT NEUF
Despite its name, Pont Neuf ("new bridge") is the oldest bridge. The first stone bridge built without houses, it's also the city's longest, widest, and is the only bridge in Paris that has never been rebuilt. Now it's conveniently outfitted with cozy stone benches so couples can admire the Seine and each other.

 A4 ✪3   ENTER AT QUAI DES GRANDS AUGUSTINS AND RUE
DAUPHINE, 1ER

MAP 3 INVALIDES

GRAND PALAIS/PETIT PALAIS

The hulking Grand Palais, an elegant art nouveau structure built for the 1900 Exposition Universelle, has one of the most spectacular interiors in all of Paris. Imagine a 335-meter (1,100-foot) glass arcade with a glass-and-iron dome at its center, along with multiple layers of balconies, and sculpture so voluptuous it seems almost flesh-and-blood. The Grand Palais is put to many uses. The Galeries Nationales host blockbuster art exhibitions, while the wing on avenue Franklin D. Roosevelt houses the Palais de la Découverte, the world's first interactive museum where demonstrations of scientific "experiments" take place several times a day. There is also a planetarium that travels back to the past and ahead to future solar and lunar eclipses – viewers can see the Paris night sky as it will look in 14,000 years.

Like its big brother, the Petit Palais was built for the 1900 Expo, but its more unified style is the work of a single architect. The facade of the not-so-petite building was influenced by the Louvre; the bas-relief shows the city of Paris protecting the arts. The "little palace" now houses the Musée des Beaux-Arts de la Ville de Paris, reopened in December 2005 after extensive

LA SEINE

The river that runs through Paris, the Seine, is itself one of the city's most memorable and romantic sights. For more than 2,000 years, Parisians have built their most impressive monuments on or near its banks, and so you can see much of Paris by boat, embarking in either a modest **Vedette (p. 81)** or one of the enormous **Bateaux-Mouches (p. 81).** Daytime rides are more popular, but a night cruise offers a romantic glimpse of the City of Light. The many bridges connecting the two banks add to the river's beauty. Among them, the **Passerelle des Arts (p. 5)** has the best views of central Paris, while **Pont Neuf (p. 5)** offers stone benches, often sought out by couples.

GRAND PALAIS   LES INVALIDES

renovations, which contains a strong collection of 19th-century artists.

 A1 ❶ 1 GRAND PALAIS: 3 AV. DU GÉNÉRAL
EISENHOWER, 8E 01-44-13-17-17   WWW.RMN.FR/
GALERIESNATIONALESDUGRANDPALAIS
HOURS: THURS.-MON. 10 A.M.-8 P.M., WED. 10 A.M.-10 P.M.

 A2 ❹ 4 PETIT PALAIS: AV. WINSTON CHURCHILL, 8E 01-44-51-19-31
WWW.PETIT-PALAIS.PARIS.FR

LES INVALIDES

In 1670 Louis XIV built this military hospital and retirement home for the soldiers who'd fought in his wars, many of whom lived in poverty. It includes the soldiers' church St-Louis-des-Invalides, lined with the captured flags of France's military campaigns, and the royal chapel Eglise du Dôme, where Napoléon's exhumed remains rest under the gilded dome in no fewer than six coffins, all enveloped in an oversize sarcophagus of Finnish red granite. Part of the Invalides complex is still used as a residence for war veterans and victims of terrorism, but it also houses the Musée de l'Armée, one of the world's largest collections of military weapons and uniforms from the Stone Age to Hiroshima, rich in Napoleonic memorabilia such as Ingres's famous portrait of him as emperor, his cocked hat and signature gray overcoat, and the fold-up bed on which he died in exile. Your ticket is also good for entrance into the adjacent Musée de l'Ordre de la Libération, which focuses on the Free French Forces and the Résistance movement during World War II, and the fourth-floor Musée des Plans-Reliefs, which contains scale models of entire French cities inside illuminated glass cases. Created between the 17th and 18th centuries and astonishingly precise, these models of fortified cities were once classified as military secrets.

 C2 ❷ 21 PL. DES INVALIDES, 7E 01-44-42-38-77   WWW.INVALIDES.ORG
HOURS: OCT.-MAR. DAILY 10 A.M.-5 P.M., APR.-SEPT. DAILY
10 A.M.-6 P.M.

MUSÉE D'ORSAY   ARC DE TRIOMPHE/CHAMPS-   TOUR EIFFEL
                   ELYSÉES

MUSÉE D'ORSAY

One of the world's great museums, the Musée d'Orsay unites many of the 19th century's most celebrated images – Manet's *Le Déjeuner sur l'Herbe,* Van Gogh's *L'Arlésienne,* Whistler's *Arrangement in Black and Gray* (Portrait of the Artist's Mother), Renoir's *Le Moulin de la Galette,* and Degas's ballet paintings. Opened in 1986, it focuses specifically on sculpture, painting, architecture, decorative arts, and photography created from 1848, the year of Marx's *Communist Manifesto,* populist revolutions, and the collapse of monarchies, up to 1914, the beginning of the Great War. The collection is housed in the soaring spaces of the old Gare d'Orsay railway station, itself a turn-of-the-20th-century work inaugurated at the 1900 Exposition Universelle. The carved limestone facade, punctuated by large clock-face windows, extends 205 yards along the Seine. On the ground floor you'll find works from the mid- to late-19th century; the middle level has art nouveau and a variety of late-19th-century works; the top floor is devoted to Impressionism and post-Impressionism. With a multitude of pieces by Van Gogh, Cézanne, Monet, Manet, Renoir, and an array of Degas bronzes, the uppermost level is the most popular. Don't miss the romantic museum restaurant on the middle level, with parquet floors, marble columns, ceiling frescoes, and views over the Seine and Tuileries Gardens.

 A5❼7 1 PARVIS DE LA LEGION D'HONNEUR, 7E 01-40-49-48-14
WWW.MUSEE-ORSAY.FR
HOURS: TUES.–WED., FRI. AND SAT. 10 A.M.–6 P.M., THURS. 10
A.M.–9:45 P.M., SUN. 9 A.M.–6 P.M.

PONT ALEXANDRE III

The gilded Pont Alexandre III was inaugurated at the 1900 Exposition Universelle in honor of the visiting czar of Russia. It has only one span and four massive columns that anchor the piers.

 B2❽8   ENTER AT QUAI D'ORSAY AND AV. DU MARECHAL GALLIENI, 8E

MAP 4 | TOUR EIFFEL/ARC DE TRIOMPHE/TROCADÉRO

ARC DE TRIOMPHE/CHAMPS-ELYSÉES

Built by Napoléon starting in 1806 to commemorate his military victories, the Arc de Triomphe was completed in 1836, after the emperor died. Elaborately decorated with statues and reliefs celebrating the battles of Austerlitz and Aboukir, the arch also protects the everlasting flame of the Tomb of the Unknown Soldier, lit on November 11, 1923. Surrounded by a swirling traffic circle called l'Etoile, the arch is accessed via an underground passage (from avenue des Champs-Elysées). Once inside, climb the 284 steps to the excellent viewing platform, which has some of the best vistas of Paris, including the Voie Triomphal extending from the Grande Arche de La Défense to the Louvre Museum.

Of the 12 roads radiating from the Arc, the busiest and best known is avenue des Champs-Elysées, which translates as Elysian Fields. The tree-lined thoroughfare is the backdrop for the annual Bastille Day Parade on July 14th, as well as the finish of the Tour de France in late July. There is little of architectural interest except for the Grand Palais on the southeast end and the Elysée Palace (the president's official residence), which is well back from the street. Instead, you'll find auto dealers, cinemas showing Hollywood blockbusters, multinational names like McDonald's and Virgin, and cafés competing to serve the world's most expensive Coke.

 A2 **2** ARC DE TRIOMPHE: PL. CHARLES DE GAULLE, 8E 01-55-37-73-77 HOURS: APR.-SEPT. DAILY 10 A.M.-11 P.M., OCT.-MAR. DAILY 10 A.M.-10:30 P.M.

 A2 **3** CHAMPS-ELYSÉES: AVE. DES CHAMPS-ELYSÉES WWW.CHAMPSELYSEES.ORG

TOUR EIFFEL

The symbol of Paris and debatably the world's most famous landmark, the Tour Eiffel (Eiffel Tower) was constructed for the Paris Exhibition in 1889 by Alexandre-Gustave Eiffel, the same engineer who created the steel skeleton for the Statue of Liberty. Not always the source of local adoration, the tower faced opposition from writers Alexandre Dumas and Guy de Maupassant, along with many other irate artists who tried to prevent its construction, protesting against "this useless and monstrous tower...dominating Paris like a black factory chimney." It was never intended to be a permanent feature of the Paris

JARDIN DES TUILERIES

OPÉRA GARNIER

skyline, but escaped being torn down in 1909 with its new role as a military radio transmitter and navigational aid for aircraft. The Tour Eiffel was the tallest building in the world until New York's Chrysler Building surpassed it in 1930. Visitors can climb the stairs to the first or second levels; take the elevator to the first, second, or top levels; or make reservations well in advance at one of the two restaurants to bypass the lines. From the top on a clear day, you can see the spire of Chartres cathedral, 89 kilometers (55 miles) away. Besides being one of the most-visited monuments in France, the tower also serves as the focal point for the elaborate pyrotechnics of the annual Bastille Day (July 14) fireworks show.

 E4 ✪35   BTWN. QUAI BRANLY AND PARC DU CHAMP DE MARS, 7E
01-44-11-23-23   WWW.TOUR-EIFFEL.FR
HOURS: JUNE-AUG. DAILY 9 A.M.-MIDNIGHT, SEPT.-MAY
DAILY 9:30 A.M.-11 P.M.

LES EGOUTS DE PARIS
A wacky and very urban tour option is a descent into the belly of one of the Second Empire's greatest inventions – a complex sewer system. Literary hero Jean Valjean (of *Les Misérables*) found an escape route here. Closed November-April.

 C5 ✪23   ENTRANCE OPPOSITE 93 QUAI D'ORSAY, 7E
01-53-68-27-81

PALAIS DE CHAILLOT
The neoclassical Palais de Chaillot was built for the 1937 Paris World Exhibition. In addition to housing a theater and two museums, the *palais* also offers some of the city's best views of the Tour Eiffel from its esplanade.

MAP4 E2 ✪32   17 PL. DU TROCADÉRO, 16E
01-44-05-72-72

TROCADÉRO
The location of the Palais de Chaillot, the hilltop Place du Trocadéro takes its name from a Spanish city captured by the French in 1823 and is the hub for six avenues that radiate out from it.

MAP4 E2 ✪31   PL. DU TROCADÉRO, 16E

MAP 5 GRANDS BOULEVARDS

JARDIN DES TUILERIES

Stretching from the Carrousel Arch at the Louvre Museum to the Place de la Concorde are the Tuileries Gardens, named for the royal palace (destroyed during the 1871 Paris Commune) that used to connect the Louvre's two western wings. The 63 acres of formal French gardens were originally created by André Le Nôtre, the landscape architect of Versailles, and feature his signature horseshoe-shaped staircase at the western end, flanked today by replicas of the *Chevaux de Marly* horse sculptures. (All of the garden's original statues are inside the Louvre, protected from the elements.)

Restored in the late 1990s, the gardens have an interesting mix of classical fountains and sculptures and contemporary art installations beneath the tree-lined alleys. This is one of the best places for people-watching in nice weather, either on a reclined park chair next to the main water fountain or at the open-air café. The garden hosts two historic buildings: the Orangerie Museum, currently closed for renovations, and the Jeu de Paume, newly opened as the National Center of Photography. Just inside the western entrance of the Tuileries is a small bookstore specializing in garden design.

 MAP 5 E3❸43 ACCESS VIA RUE DE RIVOLI AND PL. DE LA CONCORDE, 1ER HOURS: SUNRISE-SUNSET

OPÉRA GARNIER

When Emperor Napoléon III put together his building program for 19th-century Paris, the opera house was at its heart. In 1860, an unknown 35-year-old architect named Charles Garnier won the design competition over 172 competitors, promising to build "a temple to a unique art that speaks to the eyes, the ears, the heart, and the passions." However, the project was interrupted by war, politics, and flooding from an underground spring. (Garnier solved the last problem by creating an artificial lake under the opera house cellars – the phantom's hiding place in Gaston Leroux's *Phantom of the Opera*.)

Inaugurated in 1875, its opulent interior features a grand foyer with a mosaic-covered dome, a magnificent white marble staircase, and a five-level auditorium of gilt, mirrors, plaster cherubs, swan-necked partitions, and vast swaths of red velvet. In 1964 André Malraux,

France's first minister of culture, commissioned a mural by Marc Chagall to be painted on the opera's ceiling, and restoration work in the 1990s included the addition of state-of-the-art backstage equipment, fireproofing, and air-conditioning. Ballet, dance, and opera productions are performed here as well as in the Paris Opera's second venue built for the 1989 Bicentennial, the Opéra Bastille. If you just want to get a look at the magnificent interior, visit during the daytime for a solo or guided tour.

 PL. DE L'OPÉRA, 9E 01-40-01-22-63, 08-92-89-90-90
(TICKETS) WWW.OPERADEPARIS.FR
HOURS: DAILY 10 A.M.-4:30 P.M.

BIBLIOTHÈQUE NATIONALE RICHELIEU

The original national library opened in 1537, and today this architectural beauty holds Richelieu's collection of historic manuscripts, first editions, maps, medals, and stamps, which is only open to the public during special expositions.

 58 RUE DE RICHELIEU, 2E
01-53-79-59-59 WWW.BNF.FR

PLACE VENDÔME

This exclusive square created by Hardouin-Mansart in 1699 features a Napoleonic monument made from canons captured by the warring emperor. It's home to some of the most exclusive jewelry boutiques in Paris and the famous Ritz Hôtel.

 PL. VENDÔME, 1ER

MAP 6 LOUVRE/LES HALLES

MUSÉE DU LOUVRE

Built as a fortress outside the city walls in the 13th century, the Louvre was enlarged into a royal palace in the 16th century and transformed after the Revolution into a public museum in 1793. After extensive "Grand Louvre" renovations in the late 1980s and early 1990s, including the addition of I. M. Pei's 20-meter (67-foot) glass pyramid entrance and the opening of the Carrousel commercial center, the Louvre is considered the greatest museum in the world in terms of size and prestige of its collections. Well-known treasures such as the *Mona Lisa*, *Venus de Milo*, and *Winged Victory* attract the most attention, but the secret to enjoying such an overwhelming place is to pursue your own personal list of highlights. On each floor the galleries are

MUSÉE DU LOUVRE   PALAIS ROYAL

arranged chronologically and geographically, from the Far East, ancient Egypt, Rome and Greece, Islamic arts, and European paintings from the Dutch masters to the Italian Renaissance.

The free map from the information desk below the inverted pyramid at the main entrance is essential for getting around. Some lesser-visited sections of the museum are closed on a rotating basis due to lack of staff, so be sure to check the online schedule or at the information desk if you have your heart set on a particular collection.

 F2✪42   COUR NAPOLÉON, 34 QUAI DU LOUVRE, 1ER
01-40-20-50-50   WWW.LOUVRE.FR
HOURS: THURS., SAT.-MON. 9 A.M.-6 P.M., WED. AND FRI.
9 A.M-9:45 P.M.

PALAIS ROYAL
This 17th-century childhood home of Louis XIV features a peaceful garden retreat surrounded by exclusive boutiques and restaurants beneath elegant stone arcades. Adjacent to the gardens is the historic Comédie Française Theater and the bizarre striped columns of installation artist Daniel Buren, added in 1980.

 D1✪27   PL. DU PALAIS ROYAL, 1ER

TOUR DE JEAN SANS PEUR
This 15th-century Gothic turret belonged to the Duc of Burgundy, "Fearless Jean," whose assassination of the king's cousin Louis d'Orléans started the Hundred Years' War.

 B5✪8   20 RUE ETIENNE MARCEL, 2E
01-40-26-20-28

MAP 7 MARAIS

CENTRE POMPIDOU

The biggest modern-art attraction in Europe, the Centre Pompidou (or "Beaubourg" to the locals) is known for its controversial "inside-out" architecture designed by the British-Italian architects Richard Rogers and Renzo Piano. The immense exposed pipes are actually color-coded: blue for air-conditioning ducts, green for water, and yellow for electricity lines. Opened in 1970 and heavily renovated and reorganized in 2000, the building receives more than eight million visitors per year. The top three floors house the Musée National d'Art Moderne, whose grand galleries expose artworks spanning 1905 to 1960, including masterpieces by Cézanne, Picasso, Ernst, Giacometti, and Kandinsky. The Pompidou also houses four theaters for dance, music, cinema, and plays; the Public Information Library; the Industrial Design Center; and the Institute for Acoustic and Musical Research. The cavernous lobby is flanked by two mezzanines, one containing a mini-design store run by Le Printemps. Georges, the rooftop restaurant accessible from the red elevator to the left of the main entrance, has stunning nighttime views of the city. The Brancusi Atelier, a small building adjacent to the center, houses the contents of the sculptor's original studio, including tools and sculptures. Not all of the Pompidou's attractions lie within its postmodern walls – the square outside is a never-ending street party with buskers, artists, and political orators.

SIDE WALKS

When making a trip to Centre Pompidou, be sure to save time to explore the neighborhoods nearby. In the Marais, Paris's gay and lesbian district and historic Jewish center, stroll down **rue des Rosiers (p. 15),** where trendy fashion boutiques cohabitate with kosher bakeries.

Stop by **La Belle Hortense (p. 45)** on rue Vieille du Temple for a glass of wine or a book – they offer both.

The St-Paul district between the Marais and the Seine is worth a look as well, with its many hidden shops and historic monuments. The interconnecting courtyards of the **Village St-Paul (p. 62)** were once part of an orphanage. Completely restored, they now house tiny antique dealers and vintage stores.

 D2 ✪ 25 PL. GEORGES POMPIDOU, 4E 01-44-78-12-33
WWW.CNAC-GP.FR
HOURS: WED.-MON. 11 A.M.-10 P.M. (MUSEUM UNTIL 9 P.M.;
BRANCUSI ATELIER DAILY 2 P.M.-6 P.M.)

CENTRE POMPIDOU   JARDIN DES PLANTES

HÔTEL DE VILLE

This majestic City Hall, built to replace an older one destroyed by the 1871 Commune, is mostly closed to the public except for the Salon d'Accueil, which hosts free historical expositions.

 MAP 7 E2❂48   29 RUE DE RIVOLI, 4E
01-42-76-43-43

RUE DES ROSIERS

Historically the center of the Marais's large Jewish community, this narrow street is also known for its trendy fashion boutiques and predominantly gay cafés.

 MAP 7 D4❂40   RUE DES ROSIERS BTWN. RUE MALHER AND RUE VIEILLE
DU TEMPLE, 4E

MAP 8 | BASTILLE

JARDIN DES PLANTES

This immense garden surrounds the Muséum National d'Histoire Naturelle and gorgeous greenhouses. Beloved of Parisians, it showcases many tree and plant varieties, as well as a very popular labyrinth.

 MAP 8 F2❂26   57 RUE CUVIER, 5E
01-40-79-30-00

PLACE DES VOSGES

Built in 1605, the oldest square in Paris is considered a near-perfect expression of French Renaissance architecture. It's a popular place to lounge in the grass listening to musicians perform under the stone arcades.

 MAP 8 A1❂2   RUE DES FRANCS BOURGEOIS BTWN. RUE DE TURENNE AND
RUE DES TOURNELLES, 4E

MAP 9 | MONTMARTRE

SACRÉ-COEUR BASILICA

Crowning the hill of Montmartre like a giant wedding cake, the great white Sacré-Coeur Basilica is one of the city's most visible monuments. Relatively "new" on the Parisian landscape, the church was built as an "act of penance" after the catastrophic Franco-Prussian war of 1870. Work proceeded slowly, and the church wasn't finished until 1914. World War I intervened, and Sacré-Coeur was not consecrated until 1919. Unlike most other Paris monuments, the basilica isn't a beloved architectural masterpiece, and aesthetes decry its popularity as a postcard shot. Its extravagant mock Romanesque-Byzantine style was loosely inspired by the real Romano-Byzantine church of St-Front in Périgueux. Left-wing Paris has always hated the symbolism of the church, seen as a slight to the memory of the Communards, working-class radicals who seized power in Montmartre in 1871 after the Prussian siege of Paris. Protesters have invaded the church several times, and there was once an attempt to blow up one of the towers. Its location on the highest point in the city means that you'll have to climb several stairs or take the funicular to reach it. Its bell tower, 80 meters (262 feet) high, supports one of the world's heaviest bells, weighing 18.5 tons – plus another 2,000 pounds for the clapper. The interior is somewhat gloomy and decorated in neo-Byzantine mosaics.

SIDE WALKS

As one of the most popular tourist destinations in Paris, Montmartre can sometimes feel like an overcrowded victim of its own success. But step away from the tacky Place du Tertre to explore the many sights in the quiet side streets.

Tucked away among Montmartre's staircases is the café **L'Été en Pente Douce (p. 36)** and its fantastic outdoor terrace.

On the other side of Sacré-Coeur, the **Musée de Montmartre (p. 73)** was once a studio for such artists as Renoir and Utrillo. Today the 17th-century building houses a collection of paintings and memorabilia recalling the illustrious heyday of old Montmartre.

The pink and green cottage on rue St-Vincent is called the **Au Lapin Agile (p. 78),** a historic bar where Picasso and his friends used to drink. It's one of the last authentic Parisian cabarets and hosts nightly shows.

 B5✪4 35 RUE DU CHEVALIER DE LA BARRE, 8E 01-53-41-89-00
WWW.SACRE-COEUR-MONTMARTRE.COM
HOURS: DAILY 6 A.M.–10:30 P.M.

SACRÉ-COEUR BASILICA   BOIS DE VINCENNES

CIMETIÈRE DE MONTMARTRE

Take a peaceful stroll through the tranquil resting place of
luminaries like Berlioz, Fragonard, Degas, and Offenbach, and
the first great cancan star immortalized by Toulouse-Lautrec,
La Goulue.

 MAP 9 D1❸8 20 AV. RACHEL, 18E

OVERVIEW MAP

BOIS DE BOULOGNE/BOIS DE VINCENNES

Known as the "Lungs of Paris," the forests at the far
eastern and western borders of the city were created
in the mid-1800s under Emperor Napoléon III. Inspired
by the parks of London, he hired an engineer to create ornamental lakes, grottoes, waterfalls, and gardens. The Bois de Boulogne has two horse-racing tracks,
lakes for rowing, bike and horse paths, and the Jardin
d'Acclimatation, a children's amusement park with pup-
pet shows, a circus, a mini farm, a children's zoo, bum-
per cars, and trampolines. Within the bois are two
gardens: Jardin de Bagatelle, Paris's finest rose garden,
and the Pré Catalan, home to a Shakespeare garden that
doubles as an open-air theater.

The Bois de Vincennes to the east is Paris's largest for-
est, with 97 kilometers (60 miles) of paths and trails,
a romantic grotto on Lac Daumesnil, and Paris's "trot-
ting" racetrack, the Hippodrôme de Vincennes. The two
most popular attractions are the Château de Vincennes,
restored in 2004 and notable for its 14th-century dungeon and flamboyant Gothic royal chapel, and the vast
Parc Floral, a botanical garden that hosts free open-air

jazz and classical music concerts summer–fall. Walking should be avoided in both bois after sunset.

OVERVIEW MAP **C1**   BOIS DE BOULOGNE: ACCESS VIA PL. DU MARÉCHAL DE LATTRE DE TASSIGNY, 16E
HOURS: SUNRISE–SUNSET

OVERVIEW MAP **E6**   BOIS DE VINCENNES: ACCESS TO CHATEAU VIA AV. DES MINIMES, 12E 01-48-08-31-20
HOURS: SUNRISE–SUNSET

BIBLIOTHÈQUE NATIONALE MITTERRAND

Named after former President François Mitterrand in 1998, the new national library (as opposed to the 1537 Bibliothèque Richelieu) is a striking modernist monument open to visitors, with frequent exhibits and events.

OVERVIEW MAP **E5**   11 QUAI FRANÇOIS MAURIAC, 13E
01-53-79-59-59   WWW.BNF.FR

LES CATACOMBES

In the late 18th century the bones of more than six million Parisians were removed from the city's overflowing cemeteries and put on display in the quarry tunnels beneath the Left Bank. This is not for the claustrophobic!

OVERVIEW MAP **E4**   1 PL. DENFERT-ROCHEREAU, 14E
01-43-22-47-63

CIMETIÈRE DU MONTPARNASSE

This tiny cemetery is the eternal resting place for literary figures such as Baudelaire and the existentialist lovers Simone de Beauvoir and Jean-Paul Sartre. Cigarettes adorn the grave of the French bad boy of rock, Serge Gainsbourg.

OVERVIEW MAP **E3**   3 BD. EDGAR QUINET, 14E
01-44-10-86-50

CIMETIÈRE DU PÈRE LACHAISE

Over 200 years old, this enormous cemetery is as famous for its sculpted statues and sarcophagi as for its illustrious residents including Chopin, Oscar Wilde, Edith Piaf, and Jim Morrison. Be sure to get a map at the entrance.

OVERVIEW MAP **C6**   6 RUE DE REPOS, 20E
01-55-25-82-10   WWW.PERE-LACHAISE.COM

R RESTAURANTS

Hottest restaurant of the moment: **MON VIEL AMI,** p. 21

Most romantic: **LE JULES VERNE,** p. 27

Most fun: **CURIEUX SPAGHETTI BAR,** p. 33

Most quintessentially Parisian: **LE GRAND COLBERT,** p. 30

Most exotic: **LE LIVINGSTONE,** p. 31

Most original: **ANGL'OPÉRA,** p. 28

Best café: **LE ZIMMER,** p. 32

Best vegetarian options: **CAFÉ BEAUBOURG,** p. 32

Most historic: **LE GRAND VÉFOUR,** p. 31

Best splurge: **L'ATELIER DE JOEL ROBUCHON,** p. 24

PRICE KEY

$ ENTRÉES UNDER $10

$$ ENTRÉES $10-20

$$$ ENTRÉES OVER $20

MAP 1 QUARTIER LATIN/LES ILES

ATELIER MAITRE ALBERT
AFTER HOURS • CONTEMPORARY FRENCH $$$

The best dish at this chic Guy Savoy–managed rotisserie is the signature roast chicken, which is tender, meticulously cut, and served with a side of creamy mashed potatoes. Fish dishes are also consistently top-notch. The front room tends to be a little quieter.

 C4 ® 12 1 RUE MAITRE ALBERT, 5E
01-56-81-30-01

BRASSERIE DE L'ISLE ST-LOUIS *AFTER HOURS • FRENCH $$$*

This old-fashioned brasserie crams its wooden tables with diners, and its dark-wood walls reverberate with conversation. The rural atmosphere calls for rural food, in ample portions: sausages, game, pork knuckle with lentils. Finish with Berthillon ice cream.

 A4 ® 4 55 QUAI DE BOURBON, 4E
01-43-54-02-59

BREAKFAST IN AMERICA *BREAKFAST AND BRUNCH $*

Expat Craig Carlson's little Left Bank diner, where each table sports its own toaster, is a godsend for anyone experiencing IHOP withdrawal. Get your fix of fluffy pancakes with a side of bacon or scrambled eggs, or try the burgers or homemade chili later in the day.

 D5 ® 17 17 RUE DES ECOLES, 5E
01-43-54-50-28

CAFÉ DELMAS *QUICK BITES • AMERICAN $*

Previously La Chope, this café is as popular now as when Hemingway, who lived nearby, was a regular. Literary groupies and local shoppers pack the sidewalk tables, mostly drinking coffee and talking, or indulging in the dishes of the day: salads, steaks, and burgers.

 F5 ® 26 2 PL. DE LA CONTRESCARPE, 5E
01-43-26-51-26

CHANTAIRELLE *ROMANTIC • COUNTRY FRENCH $$*

Auvergne exiled to Paris, Chantairelle prides itself on its hearty dishes from the heartland, including unforgettable smoked meats that people can buy to take home. Only in France can there be this much farm in the city.

 E4 ® 19 17 RUE LAPLACE, 5E
01-46-33-18-59

LE COUPE-CHOU *ROMANTIC • FRENCH $$*

On the site of a 16th-century barbershop, this candlelit restaurant with blazing fireplaces is the perfect place for a Left Bank dinner à deux. Specials like salmon in tarragon and cream sauce or *boeuf bourguignon* add to the warming glow.

 D3 ® 16 11 RUE DE LANNEAU, 5E
01-46-33-68-69

LA GUEUZE *AFTER HOURS • BELGIAN $*

French beer is fine but Belgian beer reigns supreme. At La Gueuze,

CAFÉ DELMAS   LA TRUFFIÈRE

surrounded by stained-glass windows, you can sample almost 150 varieties from Belgium and beyond. Food has a Belgian bias, too, with the ever-popular *moules* (mussels) *marinières* a standout.

 F2 **R23** 19 RUE SOUFFLOT, 5E
01-43-54-63-00

MON VIEL AMI *HOT SPOT • FRENCH* $$$
Antoine Westermann, chef of the three-star restaurant Buereheisel in Strasbourg, brings his zesty Alsatian touch to hearty French cooking. A chic, contemporary decor adds to the restaurant's appeal.

 A5 **R5** 69 RUE ST-LOUIS-EN-L'ILE, 4E
01-40-46-01-35

LA TOUR D'ARGENT *ROMANTIC • FRENCH* $$$
The spectacular dining room of La Tour d'Argent, with views across the Seine to Notre-Dame, drips opulence, as do some of its guests. A more affordable lunchtime menu brings classics like duck à l'orange and crêpes belle époque within reach of slimmer pocketbooks.

 B5 **R10** 15-17 QUAI DE LA TOURNELLE, 5E
01-43-54-23-31

LA TRUFFIÈRE *ROMANTIC • SOUTHWEST FRENCH* $$$
Residing in a 17th-century building near the Panthéon, La Truffière focuses its attention on southwest French cooking, with truffles (naturally), goose, and duck on the menu. In winter, the roaring fire is a great asset.

 F5 **R27** 4 RUE BLAINVILLE, 5E
01-46-33-29-82

MAP 2 ST-GERMAIN-DES-PRÉS

ALCAZAR *AFTER HOURS • CONTEMPORARY FRENCH* $$
British restaurateur Terence Conran created a hit in the heart of St-Germain by combining good food, a touch of glamour, and a hot-spot bar. Sit in the airy atrium to peruse the ever-changing menu.

 C4 **R14** 62 RUE MAZARINE, 6E
01-53-10-19-99

CAFÉ DE FLORE   LES DEUX MAGOTS

AUX CHARPENTIERS   *HOT SPOT • FRENCH* $$
This fabulous old bistro, once the dining hall of an 18th-century carpenters' guild, bustles with a mix of locals who come for traditional dishes like *blanquette de veau* (veal in cream sauce), black pudding, and rabbit with rosemary and mustard.

MAP2 E3 R32   10 RUE MABILLON, 6E
01-43-26-30-05

LE BELIER   *ROMANTIC • FRENCH* $$$
If you can't afford to stay at L'Hôtel, the quirky, luxurious hostelry where Oscar Wilde famously died, give its posh restaurant a go. Order the sea bass with olive puree and sesame in a neo-baroque setting designed by Jacques Garcia.

MAP2 B2 R4   L'HÔTEL, 13 RUE DES BEAUX ARTS, 6E
01-44-41-99-00

CAFÉ DE FLORE   *CAFÉ* $$
Hemingway, Dalí, Picasso, Sartre, de Beauvoir – its list of visitors could hardly be more impressive, and the café is still the stomping ground of today's artists and philosophers, not to mention curious tourists. Bask in the sun on the street-side terrace.

MAP2 D2 R22   172 BD. ST-GERMAIN, 6E
01-45-48-55-26

LES DEUX MAGOTS   *CAFÉ* $$
A perfectly situated St-Germain café, Les Deux Magots has hosted such luminaries as Wilde, Rimbaud, Verlaine, and of course Hemingway. You can savor a coffee, take a glass of wine, or sample the café fare, from simple steaks to indulgent caviar. It's overpriced but historic.

MAP2 D2 R23   6 PL. ST-GERMAIN-DES-PRÉS, 6E
01-45-48-55-25

JACQUES CAGNA   *ROMANTIC • FRENCH* $$$
This 16th-century building on the Left Bank is home to Jacques Cagna's flagship restaurant. Start with a Breton lobster salad and work your way to the beef fillet with truffles. The bread – beautiful miniature loaves baked on the premises – is a delightful detail.

MAP2 C5 R19   14 RUE DES GRANDS AUGUSTINS, 6E
01-43-26-49-39   WWW.JACQUESCAGNA.COM

TREASURED TERRACES

Even more highly coveted than a café table in the sun is a full meal enjoyed on a pleasant terrace. Alfresco dining is a Parisian must during April–October, and to get a seat on all the top terraces, you have to reserve well in advance. The **Restaurant du Palais Royal (p. 32)** has a splendid terrace and no street noise as it faces the palace arcades, while **Café Lenotre (p. 26)** boasts an enclosed terrace in the garden section of the Champs-Elysées. There's a hidden garden terrace at the casual but modern restaurant Flora Danica (142 av. des Champs-Elysées, 8E, 01-44-13-86-26) in the Maison du Danemark on the Champs-Elysées.

LAPÉROUSE *BUSINESS • FRENCH* $$$
Try to book one of the private salons in this centuries-old restaurant, where Victor Hugo and Emile Zola used to dine. Expect classic French cuisine, such as *quenelles* (poached pike dumplings), and tuna with coriander, tomatoes, and aubergines. The Lapérouse soufflé is divine.

MAP 2 B5 **R** 8 51 QUAI DES GRANDS AUGUSTINS, 6E
01-43-26-68-04

POLIDOR *QUICK BITES • FRENCH* $
French home cooking has been the mainstay of this cozy budget bistro for more than 150 years. Humble dishes like chicken in cream sauce, curried pork, and guinea fowl with bacon simply don't go out of style. Expect shoulder-to-shoulder dining and a convivial atmosphere.

MAP 2 E6 **R** 39 41 RUE MONSIEUR LE PRINCE, 6E
01-43-26-95-34

LE RELAIS LOUIS XIII *BUSINESS • FRENCH* $$$
Once a monastery, the medieval-looking Relais makes for a sophisticated evening out and attracts well-heeled locals and visitors. Chef Manuel Martinez is celebrated for his subtle use of sauces and flavors: the lobster ravioli with foie gras and mushroom sauce is a notable example.

MAP 2 B5 **R** 7 8 RUE DES GRANDS AUGUSTINS, 6E
01-43-26-75-96 WWW.RELAISLOUIS13.COM

ROTISSERIE D'EN FACE *QUICK BITES • FRENCH* $$
In this tiny St-Germain street, Jacques Cagna opened a modest but modern rotisserie next to his three-star temple of haute cuisine. Ever popular for its reasonable prices and delicious chicken, it isn't original but it's warm and friendly.

MAP 2 B4 **R** 6 2 RUE CHRISTINE, 6E
01-43-26-40-98 WWW.JACQUESCAGNA.COM

 **MAP 3** INVALIDES

L'AFFRIOLÉ   *ROMANTIC • FRENCH* $$$

Here's a pleasant modern bistro in a quiet neighborhood that draws applause for its modern French *cuisine du marché*. That means using the freshest ingredients to turn out such dishes as spinach-and-mushroom cannelloni with ginger, and monkfish *en brochette* with eggplant and lavender.

 C1 🅡16   17 RUE MALAR, 7E
01-44-18-31-33

L'ARPÈGE   *BUSINESS • FRENCH* $$$

Chef Alain Passard is revered for his innovative food, served in elegant contemporary surroundings of smooth wood and Lalique glassware. Go for the menu surprise if you're adventurous enough to order blindly – a bavarois of avocado with pistachio oil and caviar, perhaps?

 D4 🅡32   84 RUE DE VARENNE, 7E
01-45-51-47-33 WWW.ALAIN-PASSARD.COM

L'ATELIER DE JOEL ROBUCHON
HOT SPOT • CONTEMPORARY FRENCH $$$

No reservations are taken for celebrity chef Joel Robuchon's sleek, Japanese-inspired diner, designed by Pierre-Yves Rochon, so expect a wait. Mains include chicken "cannelloni" with foie gras and morels; there are also some 30 popular starter courses. Libations include French cider and Spanish beer.

 B6 🅡13   7 RUE MONTALEMBERT, 7E
01-42-22-56-56

CAFÉ DU MARCHÉ   *CAFÉ* $

Named for the market on the same street, the café picks up the market bustle and its fresh food. Basic offerings during the day are replaced by various specials in the evening (*boeuf bourguignon*, pastas) when young locals replace the market crowd.

 D1 🅡29   38 RUE CLER, 7E
01-47-05-51-27

CHEZ L'AMI JEAN   *QUICK BITES • BASQUE* $$

With a homey tavernlike feel, this place offers a welcome break in what sometimes feels like an impersonal (if elegant) neighborhood. Step into "your friend Jean's place" and discover the warmth of the Basque country – tuna steak, duck confit, and a healthy dose of tomatoes.

 C1 🅡17   27 RUE MALAR, 7E
01-47-05-86-89

LE DIVELLEC   *BUSINESS • SEAFOOD* $$$

One of the city's best fish restaurants, Le Divellec attracts local business bigwigs and media folk to its large and well-lit dining room. Sample divine fish dishes, such as mussels with shallots and cod with caviar. Don't miss the old-fashioned dessert trolley.

 C2 🅡20   107 RUE DE L'UNIVERSITÉ, 7E
01-45-51-91-96 WWW.LE-DIVELLEC.COM

L'AFFRIOLÉ   CAFÉ DU MARCHÉ

L'EPI DUPIN   *ROMANTIC • FRENCH* $$
Innovative food and a bustling atmosphere make this small restaurant a true find. Cod with saffron leeks tastes as good as it
sounds, and the desserts, such as the apple tart, are renowned.
It's too bad it's closed on weekends.

MAP 3 D6 **R** 37   11 RUE DUPIN, 6E
01-42-22-64-56

HÉLÈNE DARROZE   *HOT SPOT • SOUTHWESTERN FRENCH* $$$
Hélène Darroze is one of the very few two-star female chefs in
Paris, and her pricey, eponymous Left Bank restaurant has earned
a strong following for its southwestern French specialties. If you're
not up for delicious but more solemn fare upstairs, try her Salon
d'Hélène downstairs, with exquisite tapas-size dishes.

MAP 3 D6 **R** 38   4 RUE D'ASSAS, 6E
01-42-22-00-11

LEDOYEN   *BUSINESS • FRENCH* $$$
The Napoléon III dining room perfectly suits the grand cooking of
Christian Le Squer, who generally presents whatever is seasonal
in two or more combinations. Sole with cucumber and ginger
mayonnaise sauce is one mouthwatering option. The bar offers a
simpler menu.

MAP 3 A2 **R** 6   1 AV. DUTUIT, 8E
01-53-05-10-00

THOUMIEUX   *ROMANTIC • SOUTHWESTERN FRENCH* $$
This is a picture-perfect bistro, with waiters in black-and-white
attire, white tablecloths, and lots of wood. The owners come from
southwest France and the cooking reflects this, with hearty dishes
such as cassoulet (a meat-and-bean casserole) and trout with
almonds.

MAP 3 C1 **R** 18   79 RUE ST-DOMINIQUE, 7E
01-47-05-49-75   WWW.THOUMIEUX.COM

MAP 4 TOUR EIFFEL/ARC DE TRIOMPHE/TROCADÉRO

ALAIN DUCASSE AU PLAZA ATHÉNÉE
BUSINESS • CONTEMPORARY FRENCH **$$$**

Superchef Ducasse has survived his move here and emerged with reputation and three Michelin stars intact. Decor mixes formal and casual – ditto the diners. His signature dish is langoustines with caviar.

 MAP 4 B5 **R18** HÔTEL PLAZA ATHÉNÉE, 25 AV. MONTAIGNE, 8E
01-53-67-65-00 WWW.ALAIN-DUCASSE.COM

ALTITUDE '95 *ROMANTIC • FRENCH* **$$$**

With a view second only to that of Le Jules Verne (one level up), Altitude '95 dishes up fine French regional cooking, such as a fish stew made with beaujolais. The dining room has a cool, metallic look, reflecting the restaurant's Eiffel Tower location.

 MAP 4 F4 **R37** FIRST LEVEL, TOUR EIFFEL, CHAMP DE MARS, 7E
01-45-55-20-04 WWW.TOUR-EIFFEL.FR

BRASSERIE DE LA POSTE *ROMANTIC • FRENCH* **$$**

The original 1920s decor has just a touch of modernity. The menu offers classic fare like cassoulet, steak, oysters, and escargots. There are no surprises, just tasty food in a buzz of conversation. The inexpensive wine list guarantees a late-night crowd.

 MAP 4 D2 **R24** 54 RUE DE LONGCHAMP, 16E
01-47-55-01-31

CAFÉ LE DÔME *CAFÉ* **$**

This is the kind of simple little café, with a view of the Eiffel Tower, that makes Paris such a delight. No wonder it attracts tourists from dawn to dusk for coffee, wine, and dishes from the all-day menu: salads, steaks, and coq au vin.

 MAP 4 E5 **R36** 149 AV. DE LA BOURDONNAIS, 7E
01-45-51-45-41

CAFÉ LENOTRE *HOT SPOT • CONTEMPORARY FRENCH* **$$$**

This rambling restaurant occupies part of a historic garden pavilion on the Champs-Elysées and boasts a beautiful terrace. There's a good penne regate with a vegetable medley and "Paris Bangkok salad" with chicken and lemongrass; for dessert, try the pink sugared almond ice cream.

 MAP 4 A6 **R15** 10 AV. DES CHAMPS-ELYSÉES, 8E
01-42-65-85-10 WWW.LENOTRE.FR

CHIBERTA *BUSINESS • FRENCH* **$$$**

Did somebody say power lunch? Guy Savoy pulls out all the stops here with such dishes as crab salad with celery, green apples, and spicy oil served in a swanky setting completely *relooké* by architect Jean-Michel Wilmotte in 2004.

 MAP 4 A2 **R1** 3 RUE ARSENE HOUSSAYE, 8E
01-53-53-42-00 WWW.LECHIBERTA.COM

LE FOUQUET'S *CAFÉ* **$$$**

There are some things you just have to do as a tourist, and having coffee on the Champs-Elysées is one of them. Fouquet's has been serving it for generations, also offering dishes named for the stars who have lingered here.

 99 AV. DES CHAMPS-ELYSÉES, 8E
01-47-23-70-60

JAMIN *BUSINESS • EUROPEAN* $$$
Gourmet food is usually served with great reverence. Not here. No fuss, no muss, just a polite professionalism to satisfy both business and leisure diners. Chef Benoît Guichard conjures magic in dishes like Dublin Bay prawn soup, Breton scallops, and wild strawberry tart.

 32 RUE DE LONGCHAMP, 16E
01-45-53-00-07

LE JULES VERNE *ROMANTIC • INTERNATIONAL* $$$
Don't let the touristy location fool you. Le Jules Verne is a great dining experience, especially if you secure a window seat in the Paris room. The menu changes constantly, roaming the world's cuisines. Romantic? Practice your proposal now.

 SECOND LEVEL, TOUR EIFFEL, CHAMP DE MARS, 7E
01-45-55-61-44   WWW.TOUR-EIFFEL.FR

MARKET *HOT SPOT • FUSION* $$$
Mix New York-based superchef Jean-Georges Vongerichten with director Luc Besson, decorate with the earthy tones of a top designer, and serve up Asian-inspired traditional dishes, like steamed cod with eucalyptus emulsion and broccoli, and you've got Market.

 15 AV. MATIGNON, 8E
01-42-63-48-18   WWW.JEAN-GEORGES.COM

PIERRE GAGNAIRE *HOT SPOT • CONTEMPORARY* $$$
Some find the minimalist surroundings too stark, others find it totally relaxing, but no one argues over the food. Gagnaire is a culinary genius, offering such creative dishes as tender white tuna in a spider-crab broth, served with baby asparagus and caviar.

 6 RUE BALZAC, 8E
01-58-36-12-50   WWW.PIERRE-GAGNAIRE.COM

LA TABLE DU LANCASTER
BUSINESS • CONTEMPORARY FRENCH $$$
Michel Troisgros's menu is organized into unusual categories: witty, zesty, sharp, and sweet. The entrées are superb and include the likes of a trio of red mullets on a bed of shredded pink grapefruit and sole meunière with coriander, clove, and giant capers. Desserts? Heavenly.

 HÔTEL LANCASTER, 7 RUE DE BERRI, 8E
01-40-76-40-76   WWW.HOTEL-LANCASTER.FR

MAP 5 GRANDS BOULEVARDS

LES AMBASSADEURS *BUSINESS • FRENCH* $$$

Its crystal chandeliers, marble, and mirrors make Les Ambassadeurs as grandly opulent as the fine hotel in which it resides. Politicians and movie moguls enjoy impeccable service and exemplary dishes, such as smoked salmon with whipped cream and caviar and the specialty chocolate tart.

MAP 5 E1 ❻37 HÔTEL DE CRILLON, 10 PL. DE LA CONCORDE, 8E
01-44-71-16-16

ANGELINA *CAFÉ • TEA* $

This tearoom is almost a century old, and so are some of its customers. The select teas come served in bone china, but the hot chocolate, made with top-quality molten chocolate, is the specialty.

MAP 5 E3 ❻41 226 RUE DE RIVOLI, 1ER
01-42-60-82-00

ANGL'OPÉRA *HOT SPOT • CONTEMPORARY FRENCH* $$$

Deconstruction is de rigueur at this upbeat restaurant where the menu is laced with entrées bearing such descriptions as broth of herbs, ginger, soft egg, and foie gras, or roasted Touquet potatoes with sweet garlic, Thai coriander, and beef. But it all comes together to delicious effect.

MAP 5 B4 ❻8 39 AV. DE L'OPÉRA, 2E
01-42-61-86-25 WWW.EDOUARD7HOTEL.COM

AUX LYONNAIS *HOT SPOT • LYONNAIS* $$

The hype was huge – superchef Alain Ducasse buys tiny bistro to preserve authentic Lyonnais cuisine – but, frankly, deserved. This early-20th-century bistro is charming, from its delightful wall ceramics, zinc bar, and homemade terrines to its excellent service and reasonable prices. It's a must.

MAP 5 A5 ❻3 32 RUE ST-MARC, 2E
01-42-96-65-04 WWW.ALAIN-DUCASSE.COM

LES BACCHANTES *AFTER HOURS • WINE BAR* $$

As the name suggests, wine is the only beverage on the menu here. It's not hard to imagine the boisterous mood in this temple to good living, where the food ranges from basic salads and charcuterie to entrecôte and pork.

MAP 5 B2 ❻5 21 RUE DE CAUMARTIN, 9E
01-42-65-25-35

LE CARRÉ DES FEUILLANTS *BUSINESS • FRENCH* $$$

Business worthies come here to impress and be impressed. Chef Alain Dutournier demonstrates his mastery of haute cuisine without losing his southwest France origins in such simple-sounding yet sublime dishes as wild hare with truffles and roast chicken with mushrooms.

MAP 5 D3 ❻32 14 RUE DE CASTIGLIONE, 1ER
01-42-86-82-82

LES BACCHANTES   DROUANT

DROUANT *BUSINESS • FRENCH* $$$

The jury of France's premier literary prize, the Prix Goncourt, meets upstairs at Drouant. The restaurant, too, could win prizes for cooking, with dishes like ravioli in truffle sauce and scallops on the half shell with salted butter.

 B4 **R**9   18 RUE GAILLON, 2E
01-42-65-15-16

L'ESPADON *ROMANTIC • CONTEMPORARY FRENCH* $$$

Romantic and grand, the Ritz has always had one of the best dining rooms in Paris. Unusual combinations, such as salmon with tomato chutney or the truffle-infused mashed potatoes, please the gourmand, while splendid desserts please just about everyone.

MAP 5 C3 **R**23   HÔTEL RITZ, 15 PL. VENDÔME, 1ER
01-43-16-30-80   WWW.RITZPARIS.COM

IL CORTILE *ROMANTIC • ITALIAN/FRENCH* $$$

In summer, Il Cortile's courtyard, complete with fountain and murals, transports you to Italy, while its food is a superb blend of Italian and French cuisine. Pasta in squid ink and strawberry soup for dessert bring in hotel residents and in-the-know locals. Be sure to book ahead.

MAP 5 C2 **R**20   HÔTEL CASTILLE, 37 RUE CAMBON, 1ER
01-44-58-45-67

LUCAS CARTON *BUSINESS • FRENCH* $$$

Chef Alain Senderens knows his market, offering a business lunch that combines value with excellence. Enjoy Breton lobster with vanilla or crab in coriander and mango in the belle epoque dining room. The sommelier will choose a wine for each course, if you wish.

MAP 5 C1 **R**15   9 PL. DE LA MADELEINE, 8E
01-42-65-22-90

LE MEURICE *BUSINESS • FRENCH* $$$

Chef Yannick Alleno is the master of this house, and what a glamorous one it is: the palace hotel's dining room was inspired by the royal apartments at Versailles. Dishes such as scallops with balsamic vinaigrette and heavenly desserts add up to an unforgettable meal.

 E3 **R**40   HÔTEL MEURICE, 228 RUE DE RIVOLI, 1ER
01-44-58-10-10

MAP 6 LOUVRE/LES HALLES

AU PIED DE COCHON   *AFTER HOURS • FRENCH* $$
This is a longtime, 24-hour Les Halles favorite, and your chance to try pig's feet – though onion soup is another house specialty.

MAP 6 C3 **R** 21   6 RUE COQUILLIÈRE, 1ER
01-40-13-77-00

BISTROT VIVIENNE   *HOT SPOT • FRENCH* $$
This bistro is an all-around pleasure – neither small, nor cavernous; comfortable but stylish; and with two terraces, one facing south onto the street, one onto the elegant Galerie Vivienne. Their *moelleux au chocolat* brings tears to a chocolate lover's eyes.

MAP 6 C1 **R** 11   4 RUE DES PETITS CHAMPS, 2E
01-49-27-00-50

LA CLOCHE DES HALLES   *QUICK BITES • WINE BAR* $
Named for the bell that used to ring to open and close Les Halles, this bistro often feels like market day as local traders and businessmen crush in to get in. It offers simple but huge and satisfying plates of charcuterie and cheese.

MAP 6 C3 **R** 19   28 RUE COQUILLIÈRE, 1ER
01-42-36-93-89

L'ESCARGOT MONTORGUEIL   *BUSINESS • FRENCH* $$$
What could be more French than a restaurant specializing in snails? Have them in mint, curried, with walnuts, or in a casserole. Charlie Chaplin and Salvador Dalí dined in this Napoléon III style bistro, which is decked with huge mirrors and crystal chandeliers.

MAP 6 B4 **R** 7   38 RUE MONTORGUEIL, 2E
01-42-36-83-51   WWW.ESCARGOT-MONTORGUEIL.COM

LA FRESQUE   *AFTER HOURS • FRENCH* $$
Like a beacon in a sea of fast-food joints and marginal cafés, this smoky Les Halles standby draws legions of young Parisians who appreciate the honest, good-value cooking the kitchen turns out on a regular basis. The homemade vegetarian tart is a perennial favorite.

MAP 6 C5 **R** 24   100 RUE RAMBUTEAU, 1ER
01-42-33-17-56

LE GRAND COLBERT   *ROMANTIC • FRENCH* $$$
Since its star turn in the movie *Something's Gotta Give* this gorgeous belle epoque brasserie has seen no shortage of Yankees, but happily its French flavor survives intact. Stick with time-honored classics like lyonnaise lentil salad, roast chicken with *frites*, and French onion soup gratiné.

MAP 6 C1 **R** 10   2-4 RUE VIVIENNE, 2E
01-42-86-87-88

LE GRAND LOUVRE   *BUSINESS • FRENCH* $$
This oasis of calm under the Louvre Pyramid offers the likes of crayfish-and-spinach salad, roast cod with sliced chorizo, and a basic beef fillet with fried potatoes. One menu category features

LE BRUNCH

For many Parisians, brunch is the most important meal of the week, in no small part because it's the least rushed. Popular brunch spots fill up fast on Sunday, and Parisians are always on the lookout for the latest trendy place to while away the afternoon over coffee, tea, juice, omelets, tarts, cakes, and more coffee. **Mariage Fréres (p. 61)** does a fancy brunch with an emphasis on exotic teas and tempting pastries, and there's no smoking. A less ceremonious but copious brunch is available at **Café Beaubourg (p. 32).** If bagels and pancakes are calling, look no further than **Joe Allen (p. 31).**

seasonally changing items inspired by food-themed works of art in the Louvre.

 F2 R41 UNDER LOUVRE PYRAMID, 1ER
01-40-20-53-41

LE GRAND VÉFOUR *ROMANTIC • FRENCH* $$$
With painted glass ceilings, mirrored walls, and 18th-century mold-ings, chef Guy Martin's haute-cuisine establishment ranks among Paris's finest dining rooms. Its broad clientele comes for the modern cuisine – ravioli stuffed with foie gras in truffle sauce, for example – and spectacular decor.

 C1 R13 17 RUE DE BEAUJOLAIS, 1ER
01-42-96-56-27

JOE ALLEN *AFTER HOURS • AMERICAN* $$
Missing home? Anyone familiar with the New York original will know what to expect: celebrity pictures on the walls, a jukebox of classics, and U.S. culinary favorites on the menu, including Louisiana fried chicken, chopped liver, and New York cheesecake.

 B5 R9 30 RUE PIERRE LESCOT, 1ER
01-42-36-70-13 WWW.JOEALLENRESTAURANT.COM

LE LIVINGSTONE *HOT SPOT • THAI* $$
Of the two hipster styles dominating the capital – cold, retro-1960s contemporary and tusked, retro-colonial lounges – the lat-ter is far more cozy. This trendy Thai place is helped by its exotic decor, even if the Africa chic doesn't quite match your sticky rice.

 E3 R36 106 RUE ST-HONORÉ, 1ER
01-53-40-80-50 WWW.LIVINGSTONE.FR

OZO *HOT SPOT • CONTEMPORARY* $$
Lots of metal surfaces lend this restaurant a New York flavor. Diners select a meat or fish, such as salmon or pork, then choose how they want it souped up. Sauces include tamarind pineapple, teriyaki, roast eggplant and coriander, and honey Thai peanut.

C6 R25 37 RUE QUINCAMPOIX, 4E
01-42-77-10-03

LE RESTAURANT DU PALAIS ROYAL *ROMANTIC • FRENCH* $$$

What could be better than strolling the historic arcades of the Palais Royal? Why, dining underneath them, of course. That proposition is made all the more appealing when the menu includes the likes of Tuscan salami with Parmesan fritters and tuna with zucchini fricassee.

MAP 6 C1 **R** 16 110 GALERIE DE VALOIS, 1ER
01-40-20-00-27

LA TOUR DE MONTLHÉRY *AFTER HOURS • FRENCH* $$

Also known as Chez Denise, this bistro is open from 7 A.M. Monday through 7 A.M. Saturday. In between, its zinc bar and tables are rarely empty. The menu is aimed at rampant carnivores. Pace yourself – portions are generous.

MAP 6 D4 **R** 29 5 RUE DES PROUVAIRES, 1ER
01-42-36-21-82

LE ZIMMER *CAFÉ* $$

This 1896 café, given a plush makeover by designer Jacques Garcia, can always be counted on for quality, copious portions of classics like goat cheese salad and French onion soup, served by friendly staff. The ample no-smoking section, with its quiet street view, deserves applause.

MAP 6 F6 **R** 45 1 PL. DU CHÂTELET, 1ER
01-42-36-74-03

MAP 7 MARAIS

L'AMBASSADE D'AUVERGNE *HOT SPOT • FRENCH* $$

This family restaurant feels more like the owner's two-story farmhouse than an eatery. Hearty dishes of pork, beef, and cabbage fill the menu. Whatever you decide on, be sure to indulge in a side order of *aligot*, a typical Auvergne-region dish made from creamy mashed potatoes mixed with mild Cantal cheese and garlic.

MAP 7 B1 **R** 6 22 RUE DU GRENIER ST-LAZARE, 3E
01-42-72-31-32 WWW.AMBASSADE-AUVERGNE.COM

BENOÎT *HOT SPOT • FRENCH* $$$

The banquettes and belle epoque surroundings make this arguably the most expensive bistro in Paris. Parisians and visitors come here in equal numbers for the *boeuf mode* (spicy beef stew) and the special blanquette.

MAP 7 E1 **R** 47 20 RUE ST-MARTIN, 3E
01-42-72-25-76

CAFÉ BEAUBOURG *BREAKFAST AND BRUNCH* $$

An excellent spot for breakfast or a late-night drink, the Beaubourg's terrace offers fantastic views of Centre Pompidou, while its interior is equally attractive. Have tea, coffee, a glass of wine, or sample the menu of steaks, sandwiches, and pastries.

MAP 7 D1 **R** 22 43 RUE ST-MERRI, 4E
01-48-87-63-96

LE ZIMMER DÔME DU MARAIS

LE C'AMELOT *ROMANTIC • FRENCH* $$

The perfect place for food-lovers, Le C'Amelot provides intimacy and indulgence with a backdrop of dim lighting and stone walls. The five-course set menu depends on the chef's daily market foray, and selections might include venison, wild boar, or artichoke soup.

MAP 7 B6 **R** 11 50 RUE AMELOT, 11E
01-43-55-54-04

CURIEUX SPAGHETTI BAR *HOT SPOT • ITALIAN* $

Is it a bar or an upscale spaghetti diner? It's both. Start with a yummy limoncello cocktail, followed by a full or half portion of spaghetti, choosing from a variety of sauces, including spicy tomato and meatball. This place is noisy but eclectic and fun.

MAP 7 D2 **R** 28 14 RUE ST-MERRI, 4E
01-42-72-75-97 WWW.CURIEUXSPAG.COM

DÔME DU MARAIS *ROMANTIC • CONTEMPORARY FRENCH* $$

This former chapel, hidden from the street, now extends more earthly offerings. The combination of setting and savor win many a diner over at this historic, domed temple.

MAP 7 C3 **R** 15 53 BIS, RUE DES FRANCS-BOURGEOIS, 3E
01-42-74-54-17

L'ETOILE MANQUANTE *CAFÉ* $

Perhaps the quintessential Marais café, this is an ideal venue to people-watch until the wee hours, as it stays open until 2 A.M. daily. There's a range of cocktails, salads, and such on offer. Don't miss the *2001 Space Odyssey*-inspired video installation in the bathrooms.

MAP 7 D4 **R** 38 34 RUE VIELLE DU TEMPLE, 4E
01-42-72-48-34

LES FOUS D'EN FACE *BUSINESS • FRENCH* $$

With a charming and funny owner, cozy dining room, and sensibly priced French fare that's always unpretentious – this is one of the few very good traditional French restaurants left in the ever-trendy Marais district. The foie gras-inflected appetizers win raves as does the garlic roast chicken.

MAP 7 E3 **R** 50 3 RUE DU BOURG-TIBOURG, 4E
01-48-87-03-75.

LE GAI MOULIN   *HOT SPOT • FRENCH* $$

Owner Christophe Violeau is a charmer, and if his friendly restaurant is always packed, it's for good reason: its very reasonably priced set menus could include anything from homemade gnocchi to *brandade de morue*, a typical French fish recipe. And there's always a buzz.

MAP **7** D2 **R** 29   10 RUE ST-MERRI, 4E
01-48-87-47-59   WWW.LE-GAI-MOULIN.COM

GEORGES   *HOT SPOT • CONTEMPORARY* $$

At dusk, the cityscape becomes a breathtaking work of art from the restaurant atop the Centre Pompidou. Prices run steep, owing more to the view and the trendy company than the curried monkfish, but a "light" menu also allows nibblers to enjoy the view.

MAP **7** D2 **R** 26   CENTRE POMPIDOU, 4E
01-44-78-47-99

PAGE 35   *QUICK BITES • CREPES* $

This modern, family-friendly restaurant in the shadow of the Musée Picasso is equal parts tea salon and creperie. Savor a salted crepe and side salad or sugared dessert crepe (the one with Brittany caramel is a winner) amid a backdrop of contemporary art for sale.

MAP **7** C5 **R** 18   4 RUE DU PARC ROYAL, 4E
01-44-54-35-35

LE 404   *HOT SPOT • MOROCCAN* $$

The French capital abounds in delicious North African restaurants, and the stylish and ever-popular "family-style Moroccan" 404, owned by the actor Momo, is one of the best. Friendly waiters navigate the tiny, packed tables and noisy crowds with couscous, tagines, and mint tea in tow.

MAP **7** B1 **R** 4   69 RUE DES GRAVILLIERS, 3E
01-42-74-57-81

LE 3   *HOT SPOT • FRENCH* $$$

Chef-owner Stéphane Moa's trendy eatery attracts an international assortment of pretty young things who come to graze on his quality, no-frills offerings that tend to be hearty, whether it's roast sea bass or a leg of lamb with *gratin dauphinois* (potatoes au gratin). Desserts are homemade and delectable.

MAP **7** D4 **R** 36   3 RUE STE-CROIX DE LA BRETONNERIE, 4E
01-42-74-71-52

MAP 8 | BASTILLE

BOFINGER   *ROMANTIC • ALSATIAN* $$

This is one of the city's most appealing old-world brasseries, with lovely art nouveau decor and heart-stopping piles of oysters in winter. Its late-night service is a hit with operagoers, who have only to cross the Place de la Bastille after the show.

MAP **8** B2 **R** 12   5 RUE DE LA BASTILLE, 4E
01-42-72-87-82   WWW.BOFINGERPARIS.COM

BOFINGER   CAFÉ DES PHARES

CAFÉ DE L'INDUSTRIE *CAFÉ* $$

Abuzz with Bastille students, artsy types, and wannabes,
l'Industrie's style lies somewhere between junk shop, bistro, and
French Colonial. The food (not that most people come here for
that) is somewhere between Paris and the French Antilles.

 A3 **R** 3   16 RUE ST-SABIN, 11E
01-47-00-13-53

CAFÉ DES PHARES *CAFÉ* $

Though the terrace overlooks Place de la Bastille, it's set back
from the worst of the traffic. You can always go inside, but on
Sundays you might get caught in the philosophy group discussion.
The menu offers coffee, beer, wine, and the usual café fare.

 B2 **R** 13   7 PL. DE LA BASTILLE, 4E
01-42-72-04-70

LE CAFÉ DU PASSAGE *QUICK BITES • WINE BAR* $

You could catch a quick bite in this cross between wine bar and
café, but the plush interior (or the secret courtyard) might tempt
you to linger. Try the andouillettes with a glass of wine for something authentic and robust.

 B4 **R** 17   12 RUE DE CHARONNE, 11E
01-49-29-97-64

CHINA CLUB *AFTER HOURS • CHINESE* $$

You can eat and drink here, but most people come to see and be
seen. Three floors of over-the-top Chinese decor begin with the
basement jazz bar, then the main-floor restaurant and bar, and
finally the upstairs chill-out bar.

 C4 **R** 21   50 RUE DE CHARENTON, 12E
01-43-43-82-02   WWW.CHINACLUB.CC

L'ENDROIT *HOT SPOT • FRENCH* $$

In French it means "the place," and it's a popular one among
locals who like being able to choose from two set menus, one
slightly fancier than the other. Expect interesting fare such as
caramelized tomato tarte tatin and minced chicken *à la vanille*.

 B2 **R** 9   24 RUE DES TOURNELLES, 4E
01-42-71-92-41

LE SOUK *HOT SPOT • COUSCOUS* $$

Low tables and cushioned benches, kilim rugs and Moroccan

ceramics, and warm colors and smells blend in this beguiling cous-cous restaurant, filled with friendly locals and some showbiz stars.

MAP 8 A4 R7 1 RUE KELLER, 11E
01-49-29-05-08

MAP 9 | MONTMARTRE

L'AUBERGE DU CLOU *HOT SPOT • INTERNATIONAL $$*
This is a perfect spot for every season, from the warming fireplace in winter to the sunny outdoor terrace overlooking stylish avenue Trudaine in summer. The hype around this hot spot is backed by authentic and original dishes.

MAP 9 E6 R31 30 AV. TRUDAINE, 9E
01-48-78-22-48 WWW.AUBERGEDUCLOU.COM

AUX NÉGOCIANTS *HOT SPOT • WINE BAR $$*
Stand at the bar with a glass of wine like the regulars do, or sit for a more substantial meal in this wonderful home-style restaurant. Food is conventional but tasty: homemade pâtés, plates of cheese, and specials of the day.

MAP 9 A5 R1 27 RUE LAMBERT, 18E
01-46-06-15-11

LE CHINON *CAFÉ $*
This laid-back café serves food until midnight and coffee, beer, wine, and hot chocolate until 2 A.M. Live music every other Sunday attracts a youngish bohemian crowd to this part of Montmartre, not yet taken over by souvenir shops.

MAP 9 D3 R12 49 RUE DES ABBESSES, 18E
01-42-62-07-17

L'ENTRACTE *HOT SPOT • FRENCH $$*
This charming, down-home bistro one block from the foot of Sacré-Coeur draws a bohemian clientele who come for the family fare, such as onion soup and steak au poivre, prepared with love and attention.

MAP 9 D5 R19 44 RUE D'ORSEL, 18E
01-46-06-93-41

L'ÉTÉ EN PENTE DOUCE *CAFÉ $*
Hidden between several sets of steep staircases, this modest café has one of the city's best outdoor terraces. The food is simple and light – but what else does one need on a warm summer's day?

MAP 9 B6 R5 23 RUE MULLER, 18E
01-42-64-02-67

LE CHINON   L'ÉTÉ EN PENTE DOUCE

OVERVIEW MAP

LA CLOSERIE DES LILAS *HOT SPOT • FRENCH* $$$
Follow greats like Picasso through these doors, which first opened
in 1808. Today La Closerie packs in hip professionals who opt for
unfussy dishes, pricey and well made. Its discreet, dark bar is a
throwback to another age.
OVERVIEW MAP **D3** 171 BD. DU MONTPARNASSE, 14E
01-40-51-34-50

GUY SAVOY *BUSINESS • FRENCH* $$$
Some have called this the best food in Paris. If truffles are on the
menu, order them. Or try the duck foie gras with sea salt and duck
jelly. The movers and shakers eat here, and the modern dining
room changes styles constantly.
OVERVIEW MAP **C2** 18 RUE TROYON, 17E
01-43-80-40-61 WWW.GUYSAVOY.COM

LES PAPILLES *HOT SPOT • FRENCH* $$$
This popular bistro – whose name means "taste buds" – has won
a loyal Parisian following for its deftly executed southwestern
French dishes such as candied pork cheek with gnocchi. Choose
a wine from the market on premises and pay only for the amount
you drink.
OVERVIEW MAP **D4** 30 RUE GAY LUSSAC, 5E
01-43-25-20-79

LE WALY FAY *ROMANTIC • AFRICAN* $$
Step off a depressing, drab street into a world of warmth, where
African fusion brings together a startling and delicious mix of
flavors from across an entire continent. The stylish, subdued restaurant also has a surprisingly tasty wine list.
OVERVIEW MAP **D5** 6 RUE GODEFROY CAVAIGNAC, 11E
01-40-24-17-79

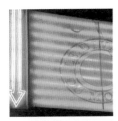

 NIGHTLIFE

Best music: **MUSIC HALL,** p. 42

Best decor: **MANDALA RAY,** p. 41

Best classic French club: **LE TANGO,** p. 45

Best gay bar: **LE DUPLEX**, p. 45

Best cocktails: **LE BAR DU PLAZA,** p. 41

Best jazz: **LE BILBOQUET,** p. 40

PIANO-VACHE *BAR*

Cheap, lively, and always flowing with rock and whatever's on tap, Piano-Vache is a well-known bar for traveling and resident youth.

 E4 **N20**   8 RUE LAPLACE, 5E
01-46-33-75-03   WWW.LEPIANOVACHE.COM

 ST-GERMAIN-DES-PRÉS

BAR DU MARCHÉ *LOUNGE*

Treat yourself to a truly Parisian address, from the Edith Piaf posters and the red banquettes to the traditionally uniformed waiters. Everyone comes here sooner or later.

 C4 **N15**   75 RUE DE SEINE, 6E
01-43-26-55-15

LE BILBOQUET *JAZZ CLUB*

The look is New Orleans red-and-black at this renowned jazz club where surprise visits by Liza Minnelli or David Bowie are always a possibility. On tap are bebop, ragtime, boogie, and blues.

 D2 **N20**   13 RUE ST-BENOIT, 6E
01-45-48-81-84

LE CAFÉ DE LA MAIRIE *LOUNGE*

Why sit inside the drab, smoky café, while Parisians flock to the terrace of this landmark? Bask in the sun or sip into the evening on the beautiful St-Sulpice square.

 E3 **N35**   8 PL. ST-SULPICE, 6E
01-43-26-67-82

CASTEL'S *CLUB*

A bastion of jet-set chic, Castel's caters to the BCBG *(bon chic bon genre,* or preppy) set. Only good luck will get you past the bouncer, unless you reserve for dinner.

 E3 **N31**   15 RUE PRINCESSE, 6E
01-40-51-52-80

LE POUSSE-AU-CRIME *BAR*

Chatty folk and friendly service bring a bevy of young travelers, students, and the congenitally social to this easygoing place.

MAP2 E3 **N33**   15 RUE GUISARDE, 6E
01-46-33-36-63

WAGG *LOUNGE*

Where Whisky à Go-go (whiskey unlimited) once stood, the stylish nightspot of British restaurateur Terence Conran keeps only the initials. Deejays spin chill-out and electronica music for pretty people.

MAP2 C4 **N16**   62 RUE MAZARINE, 6E
01-55-42-22-00

HOTEL BARS

If you're cutting costs by staying in a modestly priced hotel, splurge your spare euros on a bit of indulgent hotel bar hopping. For elegance and historic glamour, try the **Ritz's (p. 90)** swanky Hemingway Bar, named in honor of its most renowned regular, or **Le Meurice's (p. 90)** low-lit Fontainebleau Bar, with its majestic murals and leather chesterfields. The see-and-be-seen vibe is hottest at the stylish **Bar du Plaza (p. 41),** but the fickle fashion pack can also be found posing late into the night at the **Murano Urban Resort's (p. 93)** impressively long black slate bar.

MAP 3 | INVALIDES

BAR DU LUTÉTIA *LOUNGE*
Your mixed drink in this hotel bar comes steeped in history and culture. A classic literary hangout, the cool atmosphere and live piano still attract writers, politicians, and thespians.

 D6 34 HÔTEL LUTÉTIA, 45 BD. RASPAIL, 6E
01-49-54-46-09

LE CAFÉ THOUMIEUX *LOUNGE*
Dozens of vodkas can be tried at what is the defining nightspot of the 7th arrondissement. Plush red armchairs give it an old-world bordello feel; lean back and pamper yourself.

 C1 19 4 RUE DE LA COMÈTE, 7E
01-45-51-50-40 WWW.THOUMIEUX.COM

MAP 4 | TOUR EIFFEL/ARC DE TRIOMPHE/TROCADÉRO

LE BAR DU PLAZA *BAR*
This is a classic hotel bar, with comfortable chairs, wood paneling, and a modern twist that includes a bar lit from within. It's the summit of chic in a neighborhood dripping with style.

 B5 18 HÔTEL PLAZA ATHÉNÉE, 25 AV. MONTAIGNE, 8E
01-53-67-66-65 WWW.PLAZA-ATHENEE-PARIS.COM

MANDALA RAY *LOUNGE*
Trendsetters and fashion victims flock to this chic club, backed by Sean Penn and Johnny Depp, for a drink amid the lavish Asia-meets-art deco decor, fusion food, or late-night dancing.

 A4 13 32-34 RUE MARBEUF, 8E
01-56-88-36-36 WWW.MANRAY.FR

MUSIC HALL *LOUNGE*

This is one of the hippest supper club-lounge hybrids in the city, attracting the likes of Sofia Coppola, and where the tunes could range from crackling breakbeat to live opera. The high-tech, multicolored lighting system, sleek white walls, and elongated white banquettes create a modern ambience.

 B6 19   63 AV. FRANKLIN D. ROOSEVELT, 8E
01-45-61-03-63   WWW.MUSIC-HALLPARIS.COM

QUEEN *QUEER/CLUB*

The gay club for everyone, Queen has shed much of its club-elite cachet, and yet it manages to maintain its energy and produce consistently hopping crowds night after night.

 A3 7   102 AV. DES CHAMPS-ELYSÉES, 8E
01-53-89-08-90   WWW.QUEEN.FR

MAP 5 | GRANDS BOULEVARDS

BAR DE L'HÔTEL DE CRILLON *LOUNGE*

All of chic Paris seems to step through this grand hotel's gilded doors for a drink. Jazz piano provides a cool backdrop for watching old money, jet-setters, and ghetto-fabulous loungers.

 E1 37   HÔTEL DE CRILLON, 10 PL. DE LA CONCORDE, 8E
01-44-71-15-39   WWW.CRILLON.COM

BUDDHA BAR *CLUB*

Animated weekend crowds and fresh deejay mixes keep Johnny Depp's bar/restaurant buzzing. Only the giant (and impressive) bronze Buddha can stay Zen amid the hubbub.

 E1 36   8 BIS, RUE BOISSY D'ANGLAIS, 8E
01-53-05-90-00   WWW.BUDDHA-BAR.COM

CHAMPMESLÉ *QUEER*

This lesbian bar has been around since 1979, so the owner, Josy, must be doing something right. There's a cool, relaxed vibe and regular photo exhibits and cabaret evenings.

 B5 10   4 RUE CHABANAIS, 2E
01-42-96-85-20

HARRY'S NEW YORK BAR *BAR*

You can pretend you're Hemingway or another grizzled journalist newly back from the Spanish Civil War. Chances are you won't be the only one, though. Drink your Scotch straight here.

 B4 7   5 RUE DAUNOU, 2E
01-42-61-71-14   WWW.HARRYS-BAR.FR

LE CAFÉ THOUMIEUX   CAB

MAP 6 LOUVRE/LES HALLES

BANANA CAFÉ *BAR*
The mid-1990s hot spot for a mixed crowd, the Banana Café remains friendly, funky, and kitschy, and its outrageous charms are no longer the privilege of a select few.

 D5 30 13-15 RUE DE LA FERRONNERIE, 1ER
01-42-33-35-31

CAB *CLUB*
Exotic and beautiful urbanites flock to this exclusive, immense bar/restaurant that comes alive with deejay pulses. For an intimate archway table, reserve in advance and brace yourself for pricey, bottle-only orders.

MAP 6 E2 35 2 PL. DU PALAIS ROYAL, 1ER
01-58-62-56-25 WWW.CABARET.FR

LE CAFÉ *LOUNGE*
International fashion stars including John Galliano and Naomi Campbell can be spotted at this casual café, which serves up great comfort food, including chili and quiches.

 B4 4 62 RUE TIQUETONNE, 2E
01-40-39-08-00

CLUB 18 *QUEER/CLUB*
Think of this small gay dance club as the insider's Queen: the crowd is smaller and the techno music will tax the energy supply of even the hardiest disco bunnies.

 C1 14 18 RUE DE BEAUJOLAIS, 1ER
01-42-97-52-13 WWW.CLUB18.FR

LE DUC DES LOMBARDS *JAZZ CLUB*
A famous jazz haunt, the Duc welcomes international stars and local favorites. Reserve a table in advance for prime jazz-listening.

 D6 33 42 RUE DES LOMBARDS, 1ER
01-42-33-22-88 WWW.DUCDESLOMBARDS.COM

LE FUMOIR *BAR*
When not used as a canteen for the fashion shows at the

neighboring Louvre, this restaurant/bar and its cozy library draw stylish Parisians in search of a perfectly poured cocktail.

MAP 6 E3 Ⓝ 37 6 RUE DE L'AMIRAL DE COLIGNY, 1ER
01-42-92-00-24

L'INSOLITE *QUEER*

It's kitschy kitschy coo at this underground gay disco where 1970 is still going strong, although the musical menu sometimes includes 1980s hits, too. Enter through the dark courtyard.

MAP 6 C1 Ⓝ 15 33 RUE DES PETITS CHAMPS, 1ER
01-40-20-98-59

LÉZARD CAFÉ *LOUNGE*

Its prime real estate allows a nice view of strollers in the Etienne Marcel fashion ghetto. Or, as the name suggests, you may just want to bask like a lizard.

MAP 6 B4 Ⓝ 6 41 RUE TIQUETONNE, 2E
01-42-33-22-73

LE SLOW CLUB *JAZZ CLUB*

Don't be fooled by the kitschy neon sign outside – Paris's oldest jazz club has a fresh new attitude. Six nights a week are still jazz, but Sundays go hip-hop.

MAP 6 E4 Ⓝ 39 130 RUE DE RIVOLI, 1ER
01-42-33-84-30

STONEWALL *CLUB*

A deceptively narrow entry leads to a fabulous, vaulted interior, with successive rooms. One of Paris's most energetic dance clubs, it boasts a dynamic mixed crowd and talented deejays.

MAP 6 D6 Ⓝ 32 46 RUE DES LOMBARDS, 1ER
01-40-28-04-05 WWW.STONEWALL-PARIS.COM

SUNSET/SUNSIDE *JAZZ CLUB*

The tiny jazz club Sunset, a dark and intimate cellar, now has a street-level venue, Sunside. Both fill up quickly, but get there early and you can often nab a free spot.

MAP 6 D6 Ⓝ 31 60 RUE DES LOMBARDS, 1ER
01-40-26-46-60 (SUNSET), 01-40-26-21-25
(SUNSIDE) WWW.SUNSET-SUNSIDE.COM

MAP 7 MARAIS

AMNESIA *QUEER*

Amnesia is technically a gay bar, but that doesn't prevent a mixed crowd from making inroads at this upscale but accessible lounge. Of the two floors, upstairs is more spacious, but both get crowded, especially on weekends.

MAP 7 D4 Ⓝ 35 42 RUE VIEILLE-DU-TEMPLE, 4E
01-42-72-16-94

LES BAINS DOUCHES *CLUB*

Paris's most illustrious discotheque never goes out of style, keeping VIPs and name-dropping partyers alike out until dawn every night of the week.

MAP 7 B1 N 5   7 RUE DU BOURG L'ABBÉ, 3E
01-48-87-01-80

LA BELLE HORTENSE   *WINE BAR*
Feel like an old friend immediately in this small bookstore and wine bar, where vintages and titles are lovingly chosen by a discerning staff. Literary discussions flow easily at the bar.

MAP 7 D4 N 37   31 RUE VIEILLE DU TEMPLE, 4E
01-48-04-71-60

LE CAFÉ DE TRÉSOR   *LOUNGE*
One of the prime Marais terraces, the Trésor café has fixed up its interior decor. But the summer crowds don't much care, anyway, since the outdoor seating is key.

MAP 7 D4 N 39   5-7 RUE DU TRÉSOR, 4E
01-42-71-35-17

CHEZ RICHARD   *BAR*
The vibe here hovers somewhere between swanky and understated, and is living proof that there's more to the Marais than gay bars. Polite bar service is a plus.

MAP 7 D4 N 34   37 RUE VIEILLE DU TEMPLE, 4E
01-42-74-31-65

LE DUPLEX   *QUEER*
Small, smoky, arty, and so Parisian, this is a neighborhood fixture and bar with character. Expect an eclectic, mainly gay crowd, cheap drinks, and cool music that's never too loud.

MAP 7 B2 N 7   25 RUE MICHEL LE COMTE, 3E
01-42-72-80-86

MIXER BAR   *BAR*
Among the many bars in the Marais, Mixer stands out for its good music. Deejays spin the latest electro for an appropriately mixed crowd.

MAP 7 D3 N 30   23 RUE STE-CROIX DE LA BRETONNERIE, 4E
01-48-87-55-44   WWW.MIXERBAR.COM

LA PERLA   *BAR*
A Mexican restaurant of dubious authenticity, La Perla is a bustling bar for mid-twenty- and thirtysomethings with a taste for tangy margaritas.

MAP 7 E4 N 52   26 RUE FRANÇOIS MIRON, 4E
01-42-77-59-40

LE TANGO   *CLUB*
Smoky, crowded, untrendy, and very French are words that come to mind to describe this dance club known for its weekend gay balls, when all kinds of music but techno play.

MAP 7 A2 N 2   13 RUE AU MAIRE, 3E
01-42-72-17-78   WWW.TANGOPARIS.COM

MAP 8 BASTILLE

BUBAR *CLUB*

Bubar offers a rare combination in Paris – a warm welcome, sleek environs, cool jazz, tasty tapas at the bar, wines from around the globe, and no crowd. Too good to be true?

 B2 **11** 3 RUE DES TOURNELLES, 4E
01-40-29-97-72

OPA *CLUB*

This revamped industrial loft in the Bastille area is true to the neighborhood feel – decor by local artisans, an ever-varying electronic beat, art showings, and film screenings.

 C3 **20** 9 RUE BISCORNET, 12E
01-49-28-97-16 WWW.OPA-PARIS.COM

LA SCENE BASTILLE *CLUB*

This plush restaurant dance club and lounge – with lots of red and purple velvet – makes a great backdrop for electro pop and funk beats and name acts. Fridays and Sundays are gay.

 A4 **5** 2 BIS RUE DES TAILLANDIERS, 11E
01-48-06-12-13 WWW.LA-SCENE.COM

LE VIADUC CAFÉ *LOUNGE*

A mellow vibe keeps this place going long past the rest of the sleepy neighborhood – late-night snackers can dine until 3 A.M. The terrace is much coveted on summer nights.

 C5 **24** 43 AV. DAUMESNIL, 12E
01-44-74-70-70

WAX *CLUB*

Groovy girls and boys swing it in this 1960s flashback, with retro-psychedelic decor but a fast, modern beat. Deejays from the excellent dance radio FG spin on Wednesdays.

 A3 **4** 15 RUE DAVAL, 11E
01-40-21-16-16

MAP 9 MONTMARTRE

LE DIVAN DU MONDE *CLUB*

Odder than the Mad Hatter's tea party, Divan du Monde's "tea dance" draws a mix of open-minded eccentrics and hipsters who dance, watch films and performance art, and invent new pastimes.

 E5 **28** 75 RUE DES MARTYRS, 18E
01-44-92-77-66 WWW.DIVANDUMONDE.COM

L'ELYSÉE-MONTMARTRE *LIVE MUSIC*

This venue puts on festive monthly parties like a traditional village ball. Kings à l'Elysée-Montmartre is a popular techno dance night

LE DIVAN DU MONDE   FAVELA CHIC

that attracts throngs with top-notch French and international deejays.

 D6 **22** 72 BD. DE ROCHECHOUART, 18E
01-44-92-45-36 WWW.ELYSEEMONTMARTRE.COM

LES FOLIES PIGALLE *CLUB*

Plush in the way only a former cabaret and strip club can be, it gets moving after midnight. A drag-queen party every other Sunday adds girlish beauty to the capital.

 E4 **27** 11 PL. PIGALLE, 9E
01-48-78-55-25 WWW.FOLIES-PIGALLE.COM

LA FOURMI *BAR*

Its charm may be hard to define, but a mix of hard-living and better-groomed Parisians still stream in for late-night hobnob-bing – perhaps as a warm-up to neighboring clubs.

 E5 **29** 74 RUE DES MARTYRS, 18E
01-42-64-70-35

JUNGLE MONTMARTRE *CLUB*

An African-themed restaurant/bar, Jungle Montmartre serves up a lively hip-hop dance scene and killer ginger punch.

 C5 **7** 32 RUE GABRIELLE, 18E
01-46-06-75-69

LA LOCO *CLUB*

This legendary giant club is spread out over three floors, each with a different musical personality. With a maximum capacity of 2,000, there's diversity and the space to blend in.

 E2 **24** 90 BD. DE CLICHY, 18E
01-53-41-88-88 WWW.LALOCO.COM

MCM CAFÉ *CLUB*

Adjacent to the cancan classic of Moulin Rouge is this multipur-pose megacafé from the French music channel MCM – a café, res-taurant, dance club, concert hall, and TV station.

 E2 **23** 92 BD. DE CLICHY, 18E
01-42-64-39-22

LE PROGRÈS *LOUNGE*

A refuge from tourists following flags around Montmartre, this café sports a casual informality and a sleek crowd. It's a mystery how they hike up here without creasing their leather pants.

 D5 N18 7 RUE DES TROIS FRÈRES, 18E
01-42-51-33-33

OVERVIEW MAP

FAVELA CHIC *CLUB*
Claustrophobics should stay clear of this electrifying, jam-packed Brazilian restaurant and club. It has one of the best beats in Paris – down a raspberry caipirinha and start shaking.

OVERVIEW MAP C5 18 RUE DU FAUBOURG DU TEMPLE, 10E
01-40-21-38-14 WWW.FAVELACHIC.COM

NOUVEAU CASINO *MUSIC*
Behind the Café Charbon, this concert and club space hosts some of the capital's newest and best in techno, pop, and rock. It's a hub of the rue Oberkampf night scene.

OVERVIEW MAP C5 109 RUE OBERKAMPF, 11E
01-43-57-57-40 WWW.NOUVEAUCASINO.NET

LE RED LIGHT *CLUB*
This huge dance club by the Gare Montparnasse is literally underground but decidedly mainstream. Big-name deejays drop in regularly; their repertoire leans toward raging, thumping house. Red Light hosts some gay nights at least once a week.

OVERVIEW MAP D3 34 RUE DU DEPART, 15E
01-42-79-94-53

ROSEBUD *LOUNGE*
This is a living, breathing tribute to the Montparnasse feel of the 1930s-1950s: silky atmosphere, smooth music, and perfect cocktails – shaken, naturally.

OVERVIEW MAP D3 11 BIS, RUE DELAMBRE, 14E
01-43-35-38-54

 SHOPS

Most interesting perfumes: **EDITIONS DE PARFUM FRÉDÉRIC MALLE,** p. 52

Best selection of unusual books: **TASCHEN,** p. 51

Best for shabby chic decor: **BLANC D'IVOIRE,** p. 52

Best selection of gourmet goodies under one roof:
LA GRANDE EPICERIE AT LE BON MARCHÉ, p. 53

Sexiest lingerie: **SABBIA ROSA,** p. 54

Best pastry selection: **LADURÉE,** p. 54

Best place to browse during a rainstorm:
GALERIE VIVIENNE, p. 59

Best French kitchen gear: **E. DEHILLERIN,** p. 58

Best for Sunday strolling:
RUE DES FRANCS BOURGEOIS, p. 61

Best unique shirts for women: **DES PETITS HAUTS,** p. 62

MAP 1 QUARTIER LATIN/LES ILES

L'ILE FLOTTANTE *GIFT AND HOME*
Specializing in gifts, this charming boutique stocks Limoges boxes, amusing miniatures, handmade porcelain dolls, chocolates, and other fine French gourmet items.

 A5 **7** 31 RUE DES DEUX PONTS, 4E
01-43-54-69-75 WWW.LILEFLOTTANTE.COM

MARCHÉ AUX FLEURS/MARCHÉ AUX OISEAUX
GIFT AND HOME
This oft-painted flower market is one of the last in Paris. Come to enjoy the colors and fragrances any day. Songbirds join the fray on Sundays.

 A2 **3** PL. LOUIS LÉPINE, 4E

SHAKESPEARE AND CO. *BOOKS*
A landmark of literary Paris, this cultish bookstore has hosted great American expats, from the Lost Generation to today's poets. Cozy up with a book in the upstairs library.

 B2 **8** 37 RUE DE LA BÛCHERIE, 5E
01-43-25-40-93 WWW.SHAKESPEARECO.ORG

MAP 2 ST-GERMAIN-DES-PRÉS

APC SURPLUS *CLOTHING AND SHOES*
Tweed, denim, and discretion are principal components of the APC house style. The French fashion standard has this centrally located "stock" of last season's styles at 50 percent off.

 F3 **43** 45 RUE MADAME, 6E
01-45-48-43-71 WWW.APC.FR

FABRICE *ACCESSORIES AND JEWELRY*
Fabrice carries chunky, colorful, and *très* original jewelry pieces created by a mother-and-daughter team. Since 1965, their creations have graced the neck and arms of many a fashionable woman.

 C2 **12** 33 RUE BONAPARTE, 6E
01-43-26-57-95 WWW.BIJOUXFABRICE.COM

KARINE DUPONT *ACCESSORIES AND JEWELRY*
A young French designer creates the colorful, practical accessories at this boutique. Dupont's original K3 purse, with its three pockets in different sizes and colors, is often imitated, but come here to get the real thing.

 F2 **41** 16 RUE DU CHERCHE MIDI, 6E
01-42-84-06-30 WWW.KARINEDUPONT.COM

MAISON DE FAMILLE *GIFT AND HOME*
Maison de Famille carries upscale home decor and accessories

MARCHÉ AUX FLEURS   FABRICE

in the French *maison de campagne* style for those who have ever dreamed of owning a French country house.

 E4 **⑤36** 29 RUE ST-SULPLICE, 6E
01-46-33-99-91

PAUL & JOE *CLOTHING AND ACCESSORIES*
Named after the designers two young sons, this French brand is known for well-cut jeans, flowing tops, and hip little dresses for the younger crowd.

 E1 **⑤28** 66 RUE DES STS-PÈRES, 7E
01-42-22-47-01   WWW.PAULANDJOE.COM

PIERRE HERMÉ *GOURMET GOODIES*
At first glance, this gourmet patisserie looks like a jewelry boutique, with star chef Hermé's beautiful pastries lined up like gems. Look for inventive flavor combinations and seasonally changing ingredients.

 E3 **⑤34** 72 RUE BONAPARTE, 6E
01-43-54-47-77   WWW.PIERREHERME.COM

POILÂNE *GOURMET GOODIES*
In France, it's not just bread, it's "Poilâne." Although the famed baker died in 2002, his daughter has sworn to uphold the family's reputation.

 F1 **⑤40** 8 RUE DU CHERCHE MIDI, 6E
01-45-48-42-59   WWW.POILANE.FR

RUE DE RENNES *SHOPPING AREA*
Rue de Rennes is one of the major arteries in Paris's popular boutique area – with an abundance of shoe stores and convenient access to side shopping streets.

 E2 **⑤29** RUE DE RENNES BTWN. BD. ST-GERMAIN AND BD. DU
MONTPARNASSE

ST-GERMAIN *SHOPPING AREA*
Upscale shops mix with bustling cafés and bistros on this well-known boulevard. Find designer stores like Armani and Sonia Rykiel.

 D5 **⑤26** BD. ST-GERMAIN BTWN. PL. DU MONDOR AND RUE DU BAC

TASCHEN *BOOKS*
From the publishers of hip books on all matters related to art,

culture, pop culture, and lifestyle, this Philippe Starck–designed boutique is as good looking as its books.

MAP 2 C4 **S17**   2 RUE DE BUCI, 6E
01-40-51-70-93   WWW.TASCHEN.COM

VANESSA BRUNO   *CLOTHING AND SHOES*
Funky fashion for twentysomethings with fabulous figures, these pieces reconcile comfort, taste, and modernity. Bruno excels in little T-shirts, floaty layers, and asymmetric hems.

MAP 2 E4 **S37**   25 RUE ST-SULPICE, 6E
01-43-54-41-04

VILLAGE VOICE   *BOOKS*
Expat literary life pours out from the threshold of this bookstore, which offers frequent readings from British and American authors and is a major hub for anglophone Paris.

MAP 2 E3 **S30**   6 RUE PRINCESSE, 6E
01-46-33-36-47   WWW.VILLAGEVOICEBOOKSHOP.COM

MAP 3 INVALIDES

BARTHELEMY   *GOURMET GOODIES*
Considered to be the haute couture shop of French cheese, let yourself be guided by the experts into gourmet specialties such as farmhouse brie and goat cheese in olive oil, tempting your nostrils as you round the corner.

MAP 3 C5 **S25**   51 RUE DE GRENELLE, 7E
01-42-22-82-24

BLANC D'IVOIRE   *GIFT AND HOME*
Home of the elegant, yet shabby chic, aesthetic, this home-decor shop specializes in cool shades of grays and whites, on everything from furniture to linens to tabletop items.

MAP 3 D5 **S33**   104 RUE DU BAC, 7E
01-45-44-41-17

BONTON   *KIDS STUFF*
This concept store bathes the world of little ones in colorful duds and fun things for their bedrooms. The under-10s and their *mamans* will find bright, modern, and straightforward styles.

MAP 3 C5 **S23**   82 RUE DE GRENELLE, 7E
01-44-39-09-20   WWW.BONTON.FR

DEBAUVE ET GALLAIS   *GOURMET GOODIES*
Chocolate maker to kings of France and other fortunate folk for over 200 years, this historic shop serves up old-fashioned "medicinal" chocolates and delicious modern concoctions.

MAP 3 B6 **S15**   30 RUE DES STS-PÈRES, 7E
01-45-48-54-67   WWW.DEBAUVE-ET-GALLAIS.COM

EDITIONS DE PARFUM FRÉDÉRIC MALLE
BATH AND BEAUTY
Malle, the grandson of the creator of Dior perfumes, has created

VILLAGE VOICE   BARTHELEMY

an exquisite shop for his "editions" of original scents. The staff
will patiently help you find the scent right, created by one of the
shop's nine famous noses.

 C6 **S** 27 37 RUE DE GRENELLE, 7E
01-42-22-77-22 WWW.EDITIONSDEPARFUMS.COM

LA GRANDE EPICERIE AT LE BON MARCHÉ *GOURMET GOODIES*
Paris's oldest department store is as grand and captivating as
when Zola wrote about it in the 1880s. Live out your gourmet
fantasy in the cavernous grocery store (the Grande Epicerie),
adjacent to the main store.

 D6 **S** 36 38 RUE DE SÈVRES, 7E
01-44-39-81-00 WWW.LAGRANDEEPICERIE.FR

JEANNE ET JÉREMY *KIDS STUFF*
Resist the temptation to cuddle with this entire specialty shop
dedicated to teddy bears and dolls. The style is resolutely nos-
talgic, but the handmade bears are rather contemporary and
designed by artists.

 F1 **S** 41 78 AV. DE SUFFREN, 15E
01-46-33-54-54

LIBRAIRIE STUDIO 7L *BOOKS AND MUSIC*
When not designing clothing, fashion guru Karl Lagerfeld
sketches, takes photographs, and reads voraciously. This bookstore, crammed ceiling to floor with art tomes, celebrates his
inner bibliophile.

 B6 **S** 11 7 RUE DE LILLE, 7E
01-42-92-03-58

LOULOU DE LA FALAISE *CLOTHING*
This elegant collection of prêt-à-porter, jewelry, and accessories
reflect a refined fantasy world rich in color and texture, from the
former muse of Yves Saint Laurent.

 B3 **S** 9 7 RUE DE BOURGOGNE, 7E
01-45-51-42-22 WWW.LOULOU-DE-LA-FALAISE.COM

LES PRAIRIES DE PARIS *KIDS STUFF*
Mother-and-child combos from this designer as well as one-of-a-

COLETTE   HEDIARD

kind models (matching mufflers and woolen caps) have caught the
eye of fashion-wise families.

 B6 S14 6 RUE DU PRÉ AUX CLERCS, 7E
01-40-20-44-12

SABBIA ROSA *CLOTHING*

Step into this boudoir-style boutique – it feels naughty but so nice
to indulge in the flirty silk lingerie and dresses that are its trade-
mark pieces.

 C6 S28 73 RUE DES STS-PÈRES, 6E
01-45-48-88-37

SENTOU *GIFT AND HOME*

Sentou offers modern, fresh French design objects and furniture
from big interior design names and from the boutique's own label.

 C6 S26 26 BD. RASPAIL, 7E
01-45-49-00-05

MAP 4 TOUR EIFFEL/ARC DE TRIOMPHE/TROCADÉRO

CHAMPS-ELYSÉES *SHOPPING AREA*

If it's haute couture you're looking for, head to Champs-Elysées
and its side streets, avenue George V and avenue Montaigne.
This ultra-exclusive shopping quarter, nicknamed the "Golden
Triangle," is home to the top fashion houses in the city, with
designers such as Dior, Prada, and Louis Vuitton.

 A3 S8 AV. DES CHAMPS-ELYSÉES, AV. GEORGE V, AND AV.
MONTAIGNE

GUERLAIN *BATH, BEAUTY, AND SPA*

This magnificent flagship store alone may justify a trip to Paris.
You'll find rare fragrances, beauty-artist Olivier Echaudmaison's
makeup line, and the added luxury of an unparalleled day spa.

 A4 S11 68 AV. DES CHAMPS-ELYSÉES, 8E
01-45-62-52-57 WWW.GUERLAIN.FR

LADURÉE *GOURMET GOODIES*

Step back in time when you enter the gilded, sumptuous decor
at this branch of the renowned Paris tearoom. Come for lunch or

simply a pastry (more than 20 choices!), and be sure to taste one of their famous macaroon cookies.

 A4 **S12** 75 AV. DES CHAMPS ELYSÉES, 8E
01-40-75-08-75   WWW.LADUREE.FR

 MAP 5 GRANDS BOULEVARDS

ALICE CADOLLE   *CLOTHING*
Founded in 1889 by Herminie Cadolle, this boutique abounds in luxury lingerie and the movie stars who appreciate it.

 D2 **S29** 4 RUE CAMBON, 1ER
01-42-60-94-22   WWW.CADOLLE.COM

AU NAIN BLEU   *KIDS STUFF*
Opened in 1836, the Nain Bleu ("blue dwarf") was originally famous for its exquisite couture dolls and clothing; nowadays, its three stories offers a wide range of modern and old-fashioned toys.

 D2 **S28** 408 RUE ST-HONORÉ, 8E
01-42-60-39-01   WWW.AU-NAIN-BLEU.COM

CARITA   *BEAUTY*
Equally well known for hairstyling and overall beauty care, this salon offers wonderful manicures and pedicures. You'll leave feeling elegant and soigné – perfectly primed for shopping in the neighboring boutiques.

 D1 **S27** 11 RUE DU FAUBOURG ST-HONORÉ, 8E
01-44-94-11-11   WWW.CARITA.FR

CHANEL   *CLOTHING*
A classic French fashion address, Chanel has expanded its collection to include fashion-forward sportswear, but the mood remains ever elegant.

 C2 **S19** 29 RUE CAMBON, 1ER
01-42-86-28-00   WWW.CHANEL.COM

COLETTE   *GIFT AND HOME*
A trendy boutique that doubles as a museum, Colette has become a Paris style landmark for chic knickknacks and clothing for men and women. The fashionable Water Bar in the basement sells a large selection of designer water.

 D4 **S35** 213 RUE ST-HONORÉ, 1ER
01-55-35-33-90   WWW.COLETTE.FR

GALIGNANI   *BOOKS AND MUSIC*
The first English bookstore on the Continent (established 1802) offers nibbles of all subjects, in French and English, and a browser's feast of fine-art books.

 E3 **S42** 224 RUE DE RIVOLI, 1ER
01-42-60-76-07

HEDIARD   *GOURMET GOODIES*
Offering French gourmet and exotic products for more than 150 years, this upscale gastronomic boutique sells a wide range of

HERMÈS   LA MAISON DU CHOCOLAT   MAÎTRE PARFUMEUR ET GANTIER

delicious items, such as French condiments, gourmet tea, coffee, and biscuits.

  C1 **S12**   21 PL. DE LA MADELEINE, 8E
01-43-12-88-88   WWW.HEDIARD.FR

HERMÈS   *ACCESSORIES*
Famed for its signature silk scarves and ties, Hermès offers myriad delights and very expensive temptations in its large, beautifully appointed flagship store.

MAP 5 D1 **S25**   24 RUE DU FAUBOURG ST-HONORÉ, 8E
01-40-17-47-17   WWW.HERMES.COM

LAVINIA   *GOURMET GOODIES*
A mega-wine store that challenges its gourmet neighbors, Lavinia offers thousands of bottles, with an impressive selection of foreign labels, as well.

 MAP 5 C1 **S16**   3 BD. DE LA MADELEINE, 1ER
01-42-97-20-20   WWW.LAVINIA.COM

LA MAISON DU CHOCOLAT   *GOURMET GOODIES*
Chocoholics must make a solemn pilgrimage here to taste the handmade chocolates and divinely rich truffles, and to admire the artful wrapping jobs.

 MAP 5 C2 **S17**   8 BD. DE LA MADELEINE, 9E
01-47-42-86-52   WWW.LAMAISONDUCHOCOLAT.COM

MAÎTRE PARFUMEUR ET GANTIER   *BATH AND BEAUTY*
Step inside and breathe in the refinement of the Old World in this re-creation of a 17th-century perfume salon. Choose your own personal or home scents from the original line.

 MAP 5 C3 **S21**   5 RUE DES CAPUCINES, 1ER
01-42-96-35-13   WWW.MAITRE-PARFUMEUR-ET-GANTIER.COM

MARIA LUISA   *CLOTHING AND SHOES*
This stylish women's, men's, and unisex casual clothing showcases French and international designers. For more men's fashion, visit Maria Luisa Homme at 19 bis, rue du Mont Thabor.

 MAP 5 D2 **S30**   2 RUE CAMBON, 1ER
01-47-03-96-15

MINAPOE   *CLOTHING AND ACCESSORIES*
This inspired boutique is home to unique accessories and luxuri-

ous clothing designed by French/Slav Mina d'Orano. It's for trendy gals who like uncommon and imaginative pieces, often with hand-painted touches.

 C2 **S** 18   19 RUE DUPHOT, 1ER
01-42-61-06-41   WWW.MINAPOE.COM

RÉSONANCES   *GIFT AND HOME*

Carrying practical, yet fun, French home and hardware gadgets for every room in the home, Résonances is the place to find that retro kitchen utensil or timeless gift item.

 C1 **S** 14   3 BD. MALESHERBES, 8E
01-44-51-63-70   WWW.RESONANCES.FR

RUE DU FAUBOURG ST-HONORÉ   *SHOPPING AREAS*

Old French fashion houses like Hermès line this high-end shopping street – a window-shopper's paradise. Serious fashionistas find their way here.

 D1 **S** 26   RUE DU FAUBOURG ST-HONORÉ WEST FROM RUE ROYALE

SPA DES CINQ MONDES   *SPA*

No fuddy-duddy salon for pink-haired regulars, this Asian-inspired institute offers lotus flower, herbal wraps, and a delicate readjust-ment of yin and yang.

 B2 **S** 4   6 SQUARE DE L'OPÉRA LOUIS JOUVET, 9E
01-42-66-00-60   WWW.CINQMONDES.COM

TERRITOIRE   *GIFT AND HOME*

Evocative of a summer on the coast, this delightful gift shop dis-plays a breezy selection of attractive books, art objects, and more.

 C1 **S** 13   30 RUE BOISSY D'ANGLAIS, 8E
01-42-66-22-13   WWW.TERRITOIRE.COM

LA VASSELERIE   *GIFT AND HOME*

Packed with reasonably priced kitchen and home items such as porcelain mustard jars and French cheese knives, it is rare to walk out of this boutique empty-handed.

MAP 5 D4 **S** 34   332 RUE ST.-HONORÉ, 8E
01-42-60-64-50   WWW.LAVAISSELLERIE.FR

W. H. SMITH   *BOOKS*

This excellent bookstore is a locus for English-speakers in Paris and indispensable for news junkies desperate for a media fix.

MAP 5 E2 **S** 39   248 RUE DE RIVOLI, 1ER
01-44-77-88-99   WWW.WHSMITH.COM

MAP 6 | LOUVRE/LES HALLES

AGNÈS B. *CLOTHING AND SHOES*
Agnès B.'s various collections of high-quality lines for office, evening, and weekend wear sum up French style for many. Children's and men's stores are just down the street.

MAP 6 C3 S 22 6 RUE DE JOUR, 1ER
01-45-08-56-56 WWW.AGNESB.COM

UN APRÈS-MIDI DE CHIEN *ACCESSORIES*
Try on a retro feel (think 1940s), or dabble in pretty, feminine handbags and accessories at this small, original boutique. The two designers who created the label assure a strong, consistent style.

MAP 6 B4 S 5 32 RUE ETIENNE MARCEL, 2E
01-40-39-00-07

L'ARTISAN PARFUMEUR *BATH AND BEAUTY*
Specializing in fresh, original fragrances, L'Artisan is particularly prized for its selection of perfumed candles and interior scents. Stop in for a bit of sensual self-indulgence.

MAP 6 F3 S 43 2 RUE L'AMIRAL DE COLIGNY, 1ER
01-44-88-27-50 WWW.ARTISANPARFUMEUR.COM

CHRISTIAN LOUBOUTIN *SHOES*
Bring out your inner Imelda Marcos with Louboutin's beautiful, vertiginous shoes. The signature red soles and five-inch heels are pure fantasy fuel.

MAP 6 D3 S 28 19 RUE JEAN-JACQUES ROUSSEAU, 1ER
01-42-36-05-31

CINÉ MUSIQUE *MUSIC*
Look for music from your favorite film, as well as thousands of other flicks you've never heard of. The shop's owner is very knowledgeable about film soundracks and will help you find what you're seeking among the countless CDs and vinyl records.

MAP 6 E4 S 38 50 RUE DE L'ARBRE SEC, 1ER
01-42-60-30-30

DIDIER LUDOT *CLOTHING AND SHOES*
Owner Didier Ludot sells mint-condition, vintage haute-couture treasures (Chanel, Dior, Balmain, Hermès) to museums and private collectors.

MAP 6 D1 S 26 JARDIN DU PALAIS ROYALE, 24 GALERIE DE
MONTPENSIER, 1ER
01-42-96-06-56 WWW.DIDIERLUDOT.COM

E. DEHILLERIN *GIFT AND HOME*
Gourmet and novice chefs alike have been coming to Dehillerin since 1820 to stock up on professional cooking and baking equipment like piles of copper pots, casseroles, knives, gadgets, and more.

MAP 6 C3 S 20 18 RUE COQUILLIÈRE, 1ER
01-42-36-53-13 WWW.E-DEHILLERIN.FR

AGNÈS B.   L'ARTISAN PARFUMEUR

GALERIE VIVIENNE *SHOPPING AREA*
Inaugurated in 1826, this elegant covered passageway has wel-
comed tourists and window-shoppers under its glass-topped
arcade ever since. Come here to enjoy a wide range of boutiques,
a bite to eat, or just to admire the architecture.

 B1 ⑤ 1   ENTER AT 6 RUE DES PETITS CHAMPS OR 4 RUE VIVIENNE, 2E

GAS BIJOUX *ACCESSORIES AND JEWELRY*
Stop by this boutique to stock up on charming and trendy jewelry
that will add a colorful French touch to any basic outfit.

 C3 ⑤ 17   44 RUE ETIENNE MARCEL, 2E
01-45-08-49-46 WWW.GASBIJOUX.FR

LEGRAND FILLES ET FILS *GOURMET GOODIES*
Legrand is a lovely wine shop tucked into the Galerie Vivienne.
Sample the wide selection of fruits of the vine at the wine bar.

 C1 ⑤ 12   1 RUE DE LA BANQUE, 2E
01-42-60-07-12

RUE ETIENNE MARCEL *SHOPPING AREA*
Rue Etienne Marcel has become one of the hippest shopping
addresses in Paris – now a cool stretch of chic shops and urban
designer outlets.

 C3 ⑤ 18   RUE ETIENNE MARCEL BTWN. PL. DES VICTOIRES AND RUE
PIERRE LESCOT

SPA NUXE *SPA*
Treat yourself to an afternoon of pampered bliss at one of the hippest spas in the city from the French body-care line Nuxe. Asian-
inspired minimalist luxury and total discretion make it a refuge for
calm-seeking patrons.

 C4 ⑤ 23   32 RUE MONTORGUEIL, 1ER
01-55-80-71-40 WWW.NUXE.COM

STOHRER *GOURMET GOODIES*
Serving royalty alongside the common man in the same location
since 1730, this gilded, delectable patisserie is famous for creating
the Baba au Rhum pastry.

 B4 ⑤ 2   51 RUE MONTORGUEIL, 2E
01-42-33-38-20 WWW.STOHRER.FR

MAP 7 MARAIS

ANTIK BATIK *CLOTHING AND SHOES*

Step into this airy boutique for elegant and worldly duds for chic guys and gals who wish to cultivate a bourgeois bohemian look. This brand is a favorite of young, hip fashionistas.

MAP 7 D6 S 45   18 RUE DE TURENNE, 4E
01-44-78-02-00 WWW.ANTIKBATIK.FR

LES BAINS DU MARAIS *SPA*

Stepping into this Asian-inspired day spa will instantly relax you, as will their hamman (steam room) and full line of spa treatments.

MAP 7 C3 S 14   31-33 RUE DES BLANCS MANTEAUX, 4E
01-44-61-02-02 WWW.LESBAINSDUMARAIS.COM

BENSIMON AUTOUR DU MONDE *GIFT AND HOME*

Follow the rainbow of colors spread out among housewares that range from bedding, candles, and cushions to comfy clothing in natural fabrics.

MAP 7 C5 S 21   12 RUE DES FRANCS BOURGEOIS, 3E
01-42-77-16-18 WWW.BENSIMON.COM

BOUTIQUE PARIS MUSÉES *GIFT AND HOME*

This attractive shop offers an interesting selection of unique, but not touristy, gift items from a handful of Paris museums.

MAP 7 D5 S 41   29 RUE DES FRANCS BOURGEOIS, 4E
01-42-74-13-02

BRONITBAY PARIS *ACCESSORIES*

Pop into this funky Marais flagship boutique to snatch up fun, colorful leather and canvas handbags created by a French-Australian husband-and-wife team.

MAP 7 D5 S 44   6 RUE DE SÉVIGNÉ, 4E
01-42-76-90-80 WWW.BRONTIBAY.FR

CALLIGRANE *GIFT AND HOME*

Stop into Calligrane, one of the beautiful *papeteries* on this short street, for exotic papers from India or Italy and *très*-chic office supplies.

MAP 7 E4 S 53   4/6 RUE DUE PONT LOUIS PHILIPPE, 4E
01-40-27-00-74

LE CHINEUR DU MARAIS *GIFT AND HOME*

Design-oriented Parisians go crazy over collectibles from the 1950s, 1960s, and 1970s at this Marais boutique. You'll find everything from Eames chairs to funky ashtrays – and everything in between.

MAP 7 D3 S 31   13 RUE DES BLANCS MANTEAUX, 4E
01-48-04-54-46 WWW.CHINEUR-MARAIS.COM

L'ECLAIREUR (HOMME) *CLOTHING AND SHOES*

Owner Armand Hadida has an eye for the best international fash-

BENSIMON AUTOUR DU MONDE

BOUTIQUE PARIS MUSÉES

ion design. Modern styles include trendsetters such as Trussadi, Dolce e Gabbana, and Dries Van Noten.

MAP 7 D5 ⑤43 12 RUE MAHLER, 4E
01-44-54-22-11 WWW.LECLAIREUR.COM

LIBRAIRIE DES ARCHIVES *BOOKS AND MUSIC*
This bookshop specializes in new and rare art-related books – you'll find books and exposition catalogs from floor to ceiling on such topics as decorative arts, fine arts, jewelry, and fashion.

MAP 7 C4 ⑤16 83 RUE VIEILLE DU TEMPLE, 3E
01-42-72-13-58 WWW.LIBRAIRIEDESARCHIVES.COM

MARIAGE FRÈRES *GOURMET GOODIES*
Employees dressed as colonial dandies invite you to savor the scents of hundreds of excellent teas. An appropriately elegant teapot or two may be too tempting to resist.

MAP 7 D3 ⑤32 30 RUE DU BOURG-TIBOURG, 4E
01-42-72-28-11

THE RED WHEELBARROW *BOOKS*
Run by an American and Canadian team, the Red Wheelbarrow stocks all the new releases in English alongside a wide range of books for adults and children. Monthly author readings and book signings are also on offer.

MAP 7 E6 ⑤55 22 RUE ST-PAUL, 4E
01-48-04-75-08 WWW.THEREDWHEELBARROW.COM

RUE DES FRANCS BOURGEOIS *SHOPPING AREA*
This quaint shopping street in the historic Marais district provides easy access between museums and clothing boutiques. With most shops open on Sundays, it's a local favorite.

MAP 7 C4 ⑤17 RUE DES FRANCS BOURGEOIS BTWN. RUE DES ARCHIVES
AND RUE DE TURENNE

SATELLITE *JEWELRY*
Influenced by her world travels and art-collector/jewelry-making parents, Sandrine Dulon creates her timeless, unique jewelry collections twice yearly. This bright and airy boutique is full of romantic, elegant pieces.

MAP 7 D5 ⑤42 23 RUE DES FRANCS BOURGEOIS, 4E
01-40-29-45-77 WWW.SATELLITE.FR

SHINE *CLOTHING AND SHOES*
The preferred address of cutting-edge Parisians who want to dress ahead of the curve, Shine is the place to go for the very, very latest clothing and accessories.

 B4 **S** 9   15 RUE DE POITOU, 3E
01-48-05-80-10

VILLAGE ST-PAUL *SHOPPING AREA*
On the less-populated side of the Marais, this area is a quaint mini-village of 20 or so antiques and specialty shops selling 19th-century knickknacks, art deco furniture, and 1960s memorabilia, among other things. However, most are only open Thursday–Monday.

 E6 **S** 56   ENTER OFF RUE ST-PAUL BTWN. RUE CHARLEMAGNE AND
RUE DE L'AVE MARIA

 | BASTILLE

CARAVANE CHAMBRE 19 *GIFT AND HOME*
Devoted to sleep and well-being, this vast and airy shop in a former furniture warehouse offers stylish beds, linens, pj's, and all things related to the bedroom.

 B4 **S** 18   19 RUE ST-NICOLAS, 12E
01-53-02-96-96 WWW.CARAVANE.FR

DES PETITS HAUTS *CLOTHING*
This *charmant* little women's boutique specializes in the art of the T-shirt. Each season brings new colors and designs, embellished with buttons, lace, stitching, funky drawings, and more.

 A4 **S** 6   5 RUE KELLER, 11E
01-43-38-14-39

ISABEL MARANT *CLOTHING AND SHOES*
Very much in vogue with young Parisiennes, Isabel Marant is considered one of the best of the new fashion generation. Her of-the-moment styles are body-conscious and feminine.

 B4 **S** 16   16 RUE DE CHARONNE, 11E
01-49-29-71-55

LILLI BULLE *KIDS STUFF*
Shop here for fun, funky, bright, and slightly offbeat clothes created by various local designers for babies and kids. This shop on a tiny side street also carries a small selection of toys, gadgets, and furniture.

 A6 **S** 8   3 RUE DE LA FORGE ROYALE, 11E
01-43-73-71-63 WWW.LILLIBULLE.COM

MARCHÉ BASTILLE *GOURMET GOODIES*
The largest market in Paris boasts four fishmongers, three florists, and countless purveyors of juicy fresh fruits and vegetables. It's an undeniable source of color on Thursday and Sunday mornings, all year long.

MAP 8 B3 **S** 14   BD. RICHARD LENOIR AT PL. DE LA BASTILLE, 11E

DES PETITS HAUTS   MARCHÉ BASTILLE

VIADUC DES ARTS *SHOPPING AREA*
Housed in the archways below a former railway line dating from 1859, the pink brick viaduct is now home to boutiques and ateliers, all dedicated to preserving fine arts and craftsmanship. Above the viaduct, you'll find the Promenade Plantée, a 4.5-kilometer- (2.8-mile-) long garden-filled pedestrian promenade with a magnificent view of the architecture of the neighborhood.

 C4 **S** 22   1-129 AV. DAUMESNIL, 12E
WWW.VIADUC-DES-ARTS.COM

 MONTMARTRE

EMMANUELLE ZYSMAN *ACCESSORIES AND JEWELRY*
This Montmartre boutique offers a selection of up-to-the-minute fashions from French creators, as well as Zysman's line of jewelry and bags, including leather bags with flower brooches.

 D5 **S** 20   81 RUE DES MARTYRS, 18E
01-42-52-01-00

GASPARD DE LA BUTTE *CLOTHING AND SHOES*
Gaspard de la Butte followed up his children's clothes with a colorful line for women, including one-of-a-kind hand-painted pieces. It's an atelier/boutique, so you may see designers clipping and creating.

 D5 **S** 17   10 BIS RUE YVONNE LE TAC, 18E
01-42-55-99-40

L'OBJET QUI PARLE *GIFT AND HOME*
This is a charming vintage shop for picking up the retro objects one would find at a French *grand-mères*: spice jars and café au lait bowls, linens, glassware, and more.

 D5 **S** 21   86 RUE DES MARTYRS, 18E
06-09-67-05-30

L'ŒIL DU SILENCE *BOOKS AND MUSIC*
This enchanting bookshop specializes in 20th-century art books, with a selection of imports and out-of-print titles alongside the

latest ones. A selection of electro and experimental acoustic CDs rounds out the stock.

MAP 9 D4 🚇 15   91 RUE DES MARTYRS, 18E
01-42-64-45-40

PAMP'LUNE *KIDS STUFF*
Colorful inside and out, Pamp'Lune offers original and colorful clothes for the under-10 crowd. Designs steer away from the typical pink for girls and blue for boys and offers an artistic look for little ones.

MAP 9 D4 🚇 16   4 BIS RUE PIÉMONTÉSI, 18E
01-46-06-50-23

SAC ET SAC *ACCESSORIES*
Specializing in fine leather goods, this temple to the handbag also stocks French brands of shoes, accessories, and deco objects for the home.

MAP 9 D4 🚇 13   30 RUE DES ABBESSES, 18E
01-42-64-51-11

OVERVIEW MAP

LES GRANDS MAGASINS *SHOPPING AREA*
On this boulevard dedicated to French temples of fashion Galeries Lafayette and Printemps, you'll find an impressive selection of objects to desire from home to clothing to food.

OVERVIEW MAP C4   40 BD. HAUSSMANN, BTWN. RUE DE LA CHAUSSÉE D'ANTIN AND RUE DU HAVRE, 9E

LES PUCES DE ST-OUEN *GIFT AND HOME*
On the northern rim of Paris, the world's largest flea market bustles across several acres. Tourists and antiques dealers comb 15 separate markets for everything from perfume bottles to Picassos. Bargaining is expected, so plan on trying to get 20-30 percent knocked off the asking price.

OVERVIEW MAP A4   17 AV. DE LA PORTE DE CLINGNANCOURT, 18E
08-92-70-57-65   WWW.LESPUCESDEPARIS.COM

LA TUILE A LOUP *GIFT AND HOME*
For over two decades this shop has packed its shelves from floor to ceiling with French country items such as ceramics, pottery, knives, and other *arts de la table* from artisans and regions all over France.

OVERVIEW MAP D4   35 RUE DAUBENTON, 5E
01-47-07-28-90   WWW.LATUILEALOUP.COM

A ARTS AND LEISURE

Best small museum: **MUSÉE RODIN,** p. 68

Best modern art: **PALAIS DE TOKYO – SITE DE CRÉATION CONTEMPORAINE,** p. 69

Best museum gift shop: **MUSÉE DES ARTS DÉCORATIFS,** p. 70

Best for snuggling at the movies: **MK2 BIBLIOTHÈQUE,** p. 80

Best razzle dazzle: **BAL DU MOULIN ROUGE,** p. 79

Most unique variety of performances:
CABARET SAUVAGE, p. 79

Best bet for English-language theater:
THÉÂTRE NATIONAL DE CHAILLOT, p. 76

Best bike tours: **FAT TIRE BIKE TOURS,** p. 82

Best all-weather activity: **BATOBUS,** p. 81

Best family park: **PARC DE LA VILLETTE,** p. 84

MUSEUMS AND GALLERIES

 QUARTIER LATIN/LES ILES

CONCIERGERIE
Paris's first prison, the Conciergerie became notorious during the Revolution as the last stop for many before the guillotine. Marie-Antoinette's dungeon, among others, has been restored and preserved.

 A1 ❶ 1   2 BD. DU PALAIS, 1ER
01-53-40-60-93   WWW.MONUM.FR

INSTITUT DU MONDE ARABE
This Seine-side architectural wonder exhibits Arabic and Islamic art and artifacts. The building's south side is covered with shutters that open and close automatically like a camera, and the roof terrace offers great views.

 C6 ❶ 13   1 RUE DES FOSSÉS ST-BERNARD, 5E
01-40-51-38-38   WWW.IMARABE.ORG

MUSÉE NATIONAL DU MOYEN AGE – THERMES ET HÔTEL DE CLUNY
See SIGHTS, p. 2.

 D2 ❶ 14   6 PL. PAUL PAINLEVÉ, 5E
01-53-73-78-00   WWW.MUSEE-MOYENAGE.FR

 ST-GERMAIN-DES-PRÉS

MUSÉE DE LA MONNAIE
The French mint displays interesting expos on French coins and their history from Roman times to the Revolution to the present. Coins were minted here until 1973.

 B3 ❶ 5   11 QUAI DE CONTI, 6E
01-40-46-55-35   WWW.MONNAIEDEPARIS.FR

MUSÉE DU LUXEMBOURG
Next to the French Senate, facing the Jardin du Luxembourg, the museum hosts powerhouse temporary exhibits that draw crowds, like the 2005 retrospective of the painter Matisse.

F4 ❶ 44   19 RUE DE VAUGIRARD, 6E
01-42-34-25-95   WWW.MUSEEDULUXEMBOURG.FR

INSTITUT DU MONDE ARABE

MUSÉE NATIONAL DU MOYEN AGE

MUSÉE NATIONAL EUGÈNE DELACROIX

Delacroix's mid-19th-century home now exhibits his lesser-known works, enhancing the major displays in the Louvre and Musée d'Orsay.

 C3 **13**   6 RUE DE FURSTENBERG, 6E
01-44-41-86-50   WWW.MUSEE-DELACROIX.FR

MAP 3 | INVALIDES

GALERIES NATIONALES DU GRAND PALAIS

Built for the 1900 world's fair and reopened in 2005 after a 12-year face lift, the Grand Palais boasts intricate art nouveau architecture. The museum holds big-name temporary exhibits, such as an exposition on Klimt and other Austrian artists.

 A1 **2**   GRAND PALAIS, 3 AV. DU GÉNÉRAL EISENHOWER, 8E
01-44-13-17-17   WWW.RMN.FR/GALERIESNATIONALESDUGRANDPALAIS

MUSÉE DE L'ARMÉE

Specialists and laity alike should enjoy this huge collection of weaponry, armor, flags, uniforms, and other military artifacts. Many moving and beautiful objects are on display.

 D3 **30**   129 HÔTEL DES INVALIDES, RUE DE GRENELLE, 7E
01-44-42-37-72   WWW.INVALIDES.ORG

MUSÉE D'ORSAY

See SIGHTS, p. 8.

 A5 **7**   1 PARVIS DE LA LEGION D'HONNEUR, 7E
01-40-49-48-14   WWW.MUSEE-ORSAY.FR

MUSÉE MAILLOL – FONDATION DINA VIERNY

Several works by Catalan sculptor Aristide Maillol are on public display around Paris. This charming museum, opened by his muse Dina Vierny, houses more of his fine work.

 C5 **24**   59-61 RUE DE GRENELLE, 7E
01-42-22-59-58   WWW.MUSEEMAILLOL.COM

MUSÉE RODIN   PALAIS DE TOKYO

MUSÉE RODIN

Auguste Rodin's last home now houses his best works, including *The Thinker* and *The Kiss*, plus his private collection, including works by Van Gogh, Renoir, and Monet.

 D3 **Ⓐ31** 77 RUE DE VARENNE, 7E
01-44-18-61-10   WWW.MUSEE-RODIN.FR

PALAIS DE LA DÉCOUVERTE

This hands-on science museum invites the young and young-at-heart to discover starlit galaxies, microscopic worlds, and cybercultures in interactive "ateliers" for kids. It has excellent temporary exhibits.

 A1 **Ⓐ3** GRAND PALAIS, 3 AV. DU GÉNÉRAL EISENHOWER, 8E
01-56-43-20-20   WWW.PALAIS-DECOUVERTE.FR

PETIT PALAIS: MUSÉE DES BEAUX-ARTS DE LA VILLE DE PARIS

Reopened in 2005 after extensive renovations, the little brother to the Grand Palais exhibits a wide range of art from antiquity to the 20th century. It also offers workshops for children and adults.

 A2 **Ⓐ5** PETIT PALAIS, AV. WINSTON CHURCHILL, 8E
01-53-43-40-00   WWW.PETIT-PALAIS.PARIS.FR

MAP 4 | TOUR EIFFEL/ARC DE TRIOMPHE/TROCADÉRO

MUSÉE D'ART MODERNE DE LA VILLE DE PARIS

In the Palais de Tokyo, a grotesquely grand 1937 building, this 20th- and 21st-century collection includes work by Dufy, Matisse, Modigliani, and others.

 D4 **Ⓐ27** PALAIS DE TOKYO, 13 AV. DU PRÉSIDENT WILSON, 16E
01-53-67-40-00   WWW.MAM.PARIS.FR

MUSÉE DE L'HOMME

The building is uninspired but the collection is magnificent: Mayan temples, musical instruments, and Native American costumes span more than 3.5 million years of history.

 E2 **Ⓐ29** PALAIS DE CHAILLOT, 17 PL. DU TROCADÉRO, 16E
01-44-05-72-72   WWW.MNHN.FR

MUSEUMS LITE

Paris may be known for heavy-hitting museums like the **Louvre (p. 12),** but the city is also home to a wide range of interactive and unusual museums. For a hands-on experience, check out the **Palais de la Découverte (p. 68),** where you can try out a science experiment. Doll collectors may prefer the Musée de la Poupée (Impasse Berthaud, 28 rue Beaubourg, 3e, 01-42-72-73-11) and its display of hundreds of dolls in various settings. There's even a doll hospital to repair injuries. **Musée Grevin (p. 73)** delights with its eerie collection of wax figures, fun house mirrors, and mazes, as does the **Musée de la Magie (p. 71)** and its magic exhibits.

MUSÉE GALLIERA – MUSÉE DE LA MODE ET DES COSTUMES

This museum dedicated to fashion focuses on temporary expos that, for conservation purposes, display only a part of its large collection at any one time.

 C3 Ⓐ 20 10 AV. PIERRE PREMIÈRE DE SERBIE, 16E
01-56-52-86-00 WWW.PARIS.FR/MUSEES/MUSEE_GALLIERA

MUSÉE NATIONAL DE LA MARINE

The spirit of booming cannons and swelled sails is best captured in the old-ship models at this maritime history museum. Dreaming children and sailors, not landlubbers, are welcome here.

 E2 Ⓐ 33 PALAIS DE CHAILLOT, 17 PL. DU TROCADÉRO, 16E
01-53-65-69-69 WWW.MUSEE-MARINE.FR

MUSÉE NATIONAL DES ARTS ASIATIQUES – GUIMET

Some 45,000 items comprise one of the world's largest collections, with the largest Khmer collection outside Southeast Asia. In short, it's a marvel.

 D3 Ⓐ 26 6 PL. D'IÉNA, 16E
01-56-52-53-00 WWW.MUSEEGUIMET.FR

PALAIS DE TOKYO – SITE DE CRÉATION CONTEMPORAINE

Inaugurated in 2001, this lab for new art has dropped jaws, mostly over the improbable mix of shapes and sounds now dominating a warehouse-like chunk of the Palais de Tokyo.

 C4 Ⓐ 22 13 AV. DU PRÉSIDENT WILSON, 16E
01-47-23-54-01 WWW.PALAISDETOKYO.COM

LE JEU DE PAUME – SITE CONCORDE
Once the tennis court for the Tuileries Palace, this small building with spacious rooms now specializes in photography exhibitions.

 E2 38   1 PL. DE LA CONCORDE, 8E
01-47-03-12-50

MUSÉE DE LA MODE ET DU TEXTILE
At last Paris exhibits its most prized commodity: fashion. From the 17th century to present, whether powdered and petticoated, or provocative Gaultier, you'll find it here.

 E5 44   107 RUE DE RIVOLI, 1ER
01-44-55-57-50   WWW.LESARTSDECORATIFS.FR

MUSÉE DE LA PUBLICITÉ
This museum devotes itself to the "art of the ephemeral," with exhibits of posters from the 1700s to today and a most extraordinary database of promotional materials.

 E6 45   107 RUE DE RIVOLI, 1ER
01-44-55-57-50   WWW.LESARTSDECORATIFS.FR

MUSÉE DES ARTS DÉCORATIFS
Reopening in fall 2006, this museum contains decorative arts pieces from various periods and genres, including fine furniture, tapestries, and reconstructed rooms from the middle ages and Renaissance.

E6 46   107 RUE DE RIVOLI, 1ER
01-44-55-57-50   WWW.LESARTSDECORATIFS.FR

 LOUVRE/LES HALLES

MUSÉE DU LOUVRE
See SIGHTS, p. 12.

F2 42   COUR NAPOLÉON, 34 QUAI DU LOUVRE, 1ER
01-40-20-50-50   WWW.LOUVRE.FR

 MARAIS

JEU DE PAUME – SITE SULLY
This state-run site shows excellent, often controversial, photo exhibits, which have included criminal photography history, photo representations of Christ, and photographic images of World War II concentration camps.

 D6 46   HÔTEL DE SULLY, 62 RUE ST-ANTOINE, 4E
01-42-74-47-75   WWW.JEUDEPAUME.ORG

MUSÉE D'ART ET
D'HISTOIRE DU JUDAÏSME

MUSÉE DE LA MAGIE

MAISON EUROPÉENNE DE LA PHOTOGRAPHIE

This 18th-century Marais mansion and its modern annex exhibits an impressive, changing collection of photographic work, both old and new, and videography.

 MAP 7 E5 🔺 54   5-7 RUE DE FOURCY, 4E
01-44-78-75-00 WWW.MEP-FR.ORG

MUSÉE CARNAVALET

Sprawling through two beautiful Marais mansions, this museum rambles through the history of Paris in a disorganized but charming collection of paintings, fine art, and impressive furniture.

 MAP 7 C5 🔺 20   23 RUE DE SÉVIGNÉ, 3E
01-44-59-58-58 WWW.CARNAVALET.PARIS.FR

MUSÉE COGNACQ-JAY

This private collection of 18th-century fine art, donated to the state by the founders of the Samaritaine Store, reverently displays work by Rembrandt, Rubens, and Canaletto.

 MAP 7 C5 🔺 19   8 RUE ELZÉVIR, 3E
01-40-27-07-21 WWW.PARIS.FR/MUSEES/COGNACQ_JAY

MUSÉE D'ART ET D'HISTOIRE DU JUDAÏSME

In a fine 1650 Marais mansion, the story of the Jewish community in Paris and beyond is told through art and craft works, books, letters, and even anti-Semitic cartoons.

 MAP 7 C2 🔺 13   71 RUE DU TEMPLE, 3E
01-53-01-86-53 WWW.MAHJ.ORG

MUSÉE DE LA MAGIE

The young and young-at-heart will enjoy this fun collection of magic tricks and optical illusions.

 MAP 7 E6 🔺 57   11 RUE ST-PAUL, 4E
01-42-72-13-26 WWW.MUSEEDELAMAGIE.COM

MUSÉE DES ARTS ET MÉTIERS

Founded in 1794 and housed in a medieval abbey, this science museum is filled with machines, models, and automatons from 1500 to the present.

 MAP 7 A1 🔺 1   60 RUE RÉAUMUR, 3E
01-53-01-82-20 WWW.ARTS-ET-METIERS.NET

ESPACE MONTMARTRE DALI

MUSÉUM NATIONAL D'HISTOIRE
NATURELLE

MUSÉE NATIONAL D'ART MODERNE – CENTRE POMPIDOU
Spanning two floors of the Centre Pompidou, this wide collection includes good surrealist and Picasso exhibits, plus Matisse, Pollock, and a host of other style-setters.

 C2 ⓐ**12** PL. GEORGES POMPIDOU, 19 RUE BEAUBOURG, 4E
01-44-78-12-33 WWW.CENTREPOMPIDOU.FR

MUSÉE NATIONAL PICASSO
Whether you're an admirer or not, don't miss this collection of paintings, sculptures, ceramics, and drawings by the 20th century's towering genius, Pablo Picasso.

 B5 ⓐ**10** 5 RUE DE THORIGNY, 3E
01-42-71-25-21 WWW.MUSEE-PICASSO.FR

MAP 8 | BASTILLE

MAISON DE VICTOR HUGO
Formerly the great novelist's residence, this Marais mansion now houses original furniture, manuscripts, paintings, Hugo's lesser-known photographic work, and personal mementos.

 B2 ⓐ**10** 6 PL. DES VOSGES, 4E
01-42-72-10-16 WWW.MAISON_DE_VICTOR_HUGO.PARIS.FR

MAP 9 | MONTMARTRE

ESPACE MONTMARTRE DALI
Idiosyncratic and stylish, like the artist himself, this network of basement rooms displays Dali's lesser-known works, including sculptures and book illustrations. Some items are for sale.

 C4 ⓐ**6** 11 RUE POULBOT, 18E
01-42-64-40-10 WWW.DALIPARIS.COM

MUSÉE DE LA VIE ROMANTIQUE
A throwback to the time of quintessential romantics, the writers

Georges Sand and Alfred de Musset, this *hôtel particulier* (mansion) houses tidbits and artworks that are true to theme.

 F3 **32** 16 RUE CHAPTAL, 9E
01-55-31-95-67 WWW.PARIS-FRANCE.ORG/MUSEES/VIE_
ROMANTIQUE

MUSÉE DE MONTMARTRE

Once a studio for the likes of Renoir and Utrillo, this 17th-century house now displays a charming collection of documents, paintings, and memorabilia from old Montmartre.

B4 **3** 12 RUE CORTOT, 18E
01-46-06-61-11 WWW.MUSEEDEMONTMARTRE.COM

OVERVIEW MAP

FOUNDATION CARTIER POUR L'ART CONTEMPORAIN

In a building by famed French architect Jean Nouvel, contemporary art in all forms rules this space founded by Cartier's CEO – including Jean Paul Gautier's famous 2004 expo on fashion and bread.

OVERVIEW MAP **E4** 261 BD. RASPAIL, 14E
01-42-18-56-50 WWW.FONDATION.CARTIER.COM

MUSÉE CERNUSCHI – MUSÉE DES ARTS DE L'ASIE

Named after the man who donated his mansion and extensive Asian art collection to the city of Paris, this museum houses a remarkable collection of ancient Chinese art.

OVERVIEW MAP **B3** 7 AV. VÉLASQUEZ, 8E
01-53-96-21-50 WWW.CERNUSCHI.PARIS.FR

MUSÉE GREVIN

This wax museum showcases more than 300 French and international figures from showbiz, sports, political arenas, and more. Even if you don't know who all the figures are, the museum itself is a magical maze of a place, fun for both kids and adults.

OVERVIEW MAP **C4** 10 BD. MONTMARTRE, 9E
01-47-70-85-05 WWW.GREVIN.COM

MUSÉE JACQUEMART-ANDRÉ

In this magnificent 19th-century mansion, guests are privy to a private collection of works by Rembrandt, Van Dyck, and Botticelli, along with a glimpse into a grander lifestyle.

OVERVIEW MAP **C3** 158 BD. HAUSSMANN, 8E S01-45-62-11-59
WWW.MUSEE-JACQUEMART-ANDRE.COM

MUSÉE MARMOTTAN – CLAUDE MONET

Based on a vast collection bequeathed to the artist's son, this assemblage has been enhanced by other Impressionist works by Gauguin, Renoir, and Pissarro.

OVERVIEW MAP **C1** 2 RUE LOUIS BOILLY, 16E
01-44-96-50-33 WWW.MARMOTTAN.COM

MUSÉUM NATIONAL D'HISTOIRE NATURELLE

Situated in the 400-year-old Jardin des Plantes, the National Museum of Natural History consists of four historic buildings housing the museums of paleontology, botanical, mineralogy, and the stunning Grand Gallery of Evolution.

OVERVIEW MAP **D4** 36 RUE GEOFFROY-ST-HILAIRE, 5E; ACCESS GARDENS VIA QUAI ST-BERNARD, RUE BUFFON, OR RUE CUVIER 01-40-79-54-79

MUSÉE NISSIM DE CAMONDO

Set in Count Camondo's mansion on the border of the chic Parc Monceau, this museum offers a glimpse into a wealthy art collector's life at the turn of the 20th century.

OVERVIEW MAP **C3** 63 RUE DE MONCEAU, 8E 01-53-89-06-40 WWW.LESARTSDECORATIFS.FR

PERFORMING ARTS

MAP 1 QUARTIER LATIN/LES ILES

LE CHAMPO *MOVIE HOUSE*
Around since 1938, this theater plays indie/art films, plus retrospectives from some of film's biggest directors, all in VO ("*version originale,*" meaning their original language).

 MAP 1 D2 ⓐ 15   51 RUE DES ECOLES, 5E
01-43-54-51-60   WWW.LECHAMPO.COM

LE GRAND ACTION *MOVIE HOUSE*
This small chain with big screens presents new runs of old classics, brings in the best of world cinema, and puts on important retrospectives in French and English.

 MAP 1 D5 ⓐ 18   5 RUE DES ECOLES, 5E
01-43-54-47-62   WWW.LEGRANDACTION.COM

THÉATRE DE LA HUCHETTE *THEATER*
Absurdist playwright Ionesco's *The Bald Soprano* has been playing in this 85-seat theater since 1957. Also catch *The Lesson* and other Ionesco works.

MAP 1 C1 ⓐ 11   23 RUE DE LA HUCHETTE, 5E
01-43-26-38-99

MAP 3 INVALIDES

LA PAGODE *MOVIE HOUSE*
Brought to Paris a century ago, this stunning Japanese building with sumptuous silks, carvings, and paintings offers movies from the East and the West.

MAP 3 E4 ⓐ 40   57 BIS, RUE DE BABYLONE, 7E
01-45-55-48-48

MAP 4 TOUR EIFFEL/ARC DE TRIOMPHE/TROCADÉRO

CINÉMA LE BALZAC *MOVIE HOUSE*
This art deco showcase just off the Champs-Elysées often hosts film premieres. It also shows the latest international hits and

THÉÂTRE NATIONAL DE CHAILLOT   L'OLYMPIA

mounts silent films accompanied by live music on the second Sunday of every month at 11 A.M.

 A3 **4** 1 RUE BALZAC, 8E
01-45-61-10-60   WWW.CINEMABALZAC.COM

LE LIDO *CABARET*
Since 1946, this family-owned cabaret has been putting on the glitz with its elaborate shows and risqué showgirls (some are top-less). Partly cheesy, partly over-the-top, it's definitely a "must-do" for first-timers in Paris.

 A3 **6** 116 BIS AV. DES CHAMPS-ELYSÉES, 8E
01-40-76-56-10   WWW.LIDO.FR

THÉÂTRE DES CHAMPS-ELYSÉES *CONCERTS*
Stravinsky's *Rite of Spring* debuted here, and this lovely old the-ater still puts on concerts and recitals by world-renowned artists and orchestras.

 C4 **21** 15 AV. MONTAIGNE, 8E
01-49-52-50-00   WWW.THEATRECHAMPSELYSEES.FR

THÉÂTRE NATIONAL DE CHAILLOT *THEATER*
Non-francophones will enjoy the translation system in this 1930s the-ater, which hosts large-scale musicals and other grand productions.

 E2 **30** 1 PL. TROCADÉRO, 16E
01-53-65-31-00   WWW.THEATRE-CHAILLOT.FR

MAP 5 | GRANDS BOULEVARDS

L'OLYMPIA *THEATER/CONCERTS*
Once a music hall, then a concert venue (the Beatles played here), l'Olympia is now home to a range of music and drama productions.

 B2 **6** 28 BD. DES CAPUCINES, 2E
08-92-68-33-68   WWW.OLYMPIAHALL.COM

OPÉRA GARNIER
See SIGHTS, p. 11.

 A3 **2** PL. DE L'OPÉRA, 9E
01-40-01-22-63, 08-92-89-90-90 (TICKETS)
WWW.OPERADEPARIS.FR

MAP 6 LOUVRE/LES HALLES

COMÉDIE FRANÇAISE (SALLE RICHELIEU) *THEATER*

Based here for more than 200 years, France's oldest theater company puts on the grand classics of French and international drama.

 E1◑34 2 RUE DE RICHELIEU, 1ER
08-25-10-16-80 WWW.COMEDIE-FRANCAISE.FR

THÉÂTRE DE LA VILLE *DANCE*

This city-owned venue primarily hosts dance, with star choreographers like Pina Bausch appearing. It also puts on contemporary drama and world music concerts.

 F6◑47 2 PL. DU CHÂTELET, 4E
01-42-74-22-77 WWW.THEATREDELAVILLE-PARIS.COM

THÉÂTRE MUSICAL DE PARIS *BALLET/CONCERTS*

Known as "the Châtelet" for its location, the home of Diaghilev mixes world-class ballet, music, and opera. Visit Sunday mornings for the chamber music and certain weekdays at lunchtime for special concerts.

 F6◑46 1 PL. DU CHÂTELET, 1ER
01-40-28-28-40 WWW.CHATELET-THEATRE.COM

MAP 7 MARAIS

CAFÉ DE LA GARE *VARIOUS*

If you want to sample Paris's café-theater scene, this Marais

---

GOING TO THE MOVIES

With more than 700 movies a year shot in the City of Light, you may just stumble across a movie shoot in progress. However, a more sure-fire way to see your favorite stars is to visit one of the big screens in Paris. Check local entertainment guides for films listed as "VO" *(version originale)* to make sure the Anglophone flick you have chosen is in English. Then make sure you get the right popcorn – Parisians get a choice of salty *(salée)* or sweet *(sucré)*. Or perhaps you'd prefer an ice cream cone or a beer. Last but not least, choose your theater: **La Pagode (p. 75)** for a world film perhaps, **Le Grand Rex (p. 79)** for a big blockbuster, or the **MK2 Bibliothèque (p. 80)** for its seats built for two.

OPÉRA NATIONAL DE PARIS BASTILLE   LES ABBESSES

courtyard setting is one of the best, with offerings of drama, comedy, cabaret, and stand-up.

 D2 🅐27 41 RUE DU TEMPLE, 4E
01-42-78-52-51 WWW.CAFE-DE-LA-GARE.FR.ST

IRCAM *CONCERTS*
In this unattractive offshoot of the Centre Pompidou that focuses on musical creation and research, enjoy an eclectic range of music from some promising, often experimental, up-and-comers. It also offers opera, films, and debates.

 D1 🅐23 1 PL. IGOR STRAVINSKY, 4E
01-44-78-48-43 WWW.IRCAM.FR

MAP 8 | BASTILLE

OPÉRA NATIONAL DE PARIS BASTILLE *OPERA/CONCERTS*
Opened in 1989 to enhance the Garnier, this theater lacks the soul of the original, but presents top-notch opera, symphony, and ballet. Performances take place September through mid-July.

 B3 🅐15 120 RUE DE LYON AT PL. DE LA BASTILLE, 12E
01-40-01-17-89 WWW.OPERADEPARIS.FR

MAP 9 | MONTMARTRE

LES ABBESSES *VARIOUS*
Modern drama, dance, and world music productions share the stage in this neoclassical theater and second home to Théâtre de la Ville.

 D4 🅐14 31 RUE DES ABBESSES, 18E
01-42-74-22-77 WWW.THEATREDELAVILLE-PARIS.COM

AU LAPIN AGILE *CABARET*
The setting in Steve Martin's fictional play about Picasso, this atmospheric, legendary Montmartre cabaret may not spell a wild

night out, but it's a great place to hear old French *chansons* sung by an enthusiastic group of young singers.

 B3 A2 22 RUE DES SAULES, 18E
01-46-06-85-87 WWW.AU-LAPIN-AGILE.COM

BAL DU MOULIN ROUGE *CABARET*
Drink in the razzle-dazzle, which shimmers even without Nicole Kidman. The real thing lacks some of the film's pizzazz – but how can 1,000 sequined and feathered costumes go wrong?

 E2 A25 82 BD. DE CLICHY, 18E
01-53-09-82-82 WWW.MOULINROUGE.FR

LA CIGALE *CABARET*
This cabaret theater first opened in 1887 and it has presented a broad mix of music and drama ever since. It was renovated in the late 1980s by French designer Philippe Starck.

 E5 A30 120 BD. DE ROCHECHOUART, 18E
01-46-06-59-29 OR 01-49-25-89-99 (TICKETS)
WWW.LACIGALE.FR

LE STUDIO 28 *MOVIE HOUSE*
Dali paintings once graced the foyer of this historic Montmartre venue, which mixes movie classics with the latest from cult directors.

 D3 A10 10 RUE THOLOZÉ, 18E
01-46-06-36-07 WWW.CINEMASTUDIO28.COM

OVERVIEW MAP

CABARET SAUVAGE *CABARET*
Artists from all over the world perform concerts, cabaret shows, and more under the big circus tent at the Cabarat Sauvage in a setting that is purely magical with its red velvet chairs and sparkling lights.

OVERVIEW MAP B5 PEDESTRIAN ACCESS AT 59 BD. MACDONALD IN
PARC DE LA VILLETTE, 19E
01-42-09-03-09 WWW.CABARETSAUVAGE.COM

CITÉ DE LA MUSIQUE *CONCERTS*
Part of Parc de la Villette, this music complex hosts concerts and performances of dazzling variety, from a famed jazz festival in July to world music concerts.

OVERVIEW MAP B5 221 AV. JEAN JAURÉS, 19E
01-44-84-44-84 WWW.CITE-MUSIQUE.FR

LE GRAND REX *MOVIE HOUSE*
Open since 1932, one of the biggest cinemas in Europe hosts movies, premieres, big-name concerts, and more. It also offers guided tours of the theater, some combining visits to other tourist sites or special courses for children.

OVERVIEW MAP C4 1 BD. POISSONIÈRE, 2E
08-92-68-05-96 WWW.LEGRANDREX.COM

BAL DU MOULIN ROUGE   MK2 BIBLIOTHÈQUE

MK2 BIBLIOTHÈQUE *MOVIE HOUSE*

A French-style multiplex cinema complete with great extras such
as a DVD boutique, a classical/world music shop, and cool cafés.
Watch a film in the modern theaters filled with cozy red love seats
for two.

OVERVIEW MAP E5   128/162 AV. DE FRANCE, 13E
08-92-69-84-84 WWW.MK2.COM

THÉÂTRE DE LA BASTILLE *DANCE*

This is one of the city's leading dance venues for cutting-edge
contemporary work, experimental music, and drama.

OVERVIEW MAP D5   76 RUE DE LA ROQUETTE, 11E
01-43-57-42-14 WWW.THEATRE-BASTILLE.COM

RECREATION

 2 ST-GERMAIN-DES-PRÉS

VEDETTES DU PONT NEUF
Holding up to 500 passengers at a time (smaller than the Bateaux-Mouches), these Seine cruises let you see many Paris sights by boat with an in-person commentator.

 A3 SQUARE DU VERT GALANT (BENEATH PONT NEUF), 1ER
01-46-33-98-38 WWW.VEDETTESDUPONTNEUF.COM

 4 TOUR EIFFEL/ARC DE TRIOMPHE/TROCADÉRO

BATEAUX-MOUCHES
With capacities of 600-1,400 passengers, these large boats offer both day and night cruises of the Seine with recorded commentary in multiple languages.

 D4 PONT DE L'ALMA, 7E
01-40-76-99-99 WWW.BATEAUX-MOUCHES.FR

BATOBUS
Hop on and hop off at various sights with a day pass for this commuter boat used by Parisians. Unlike boat cruises, these are commentary free, which can be a blessing. Stops include the Tour Eiffel, Musée d'Orsay, Louvre, Notre-Dame, and Jardin des Plantes.

 E3 34 PORT DE LA BOURDONNAIS, 7E
01-44-11-33-99 WWW.BATOBUS.COM

 7 MARAIS

PARIS RANDO VÉLO
This volunteer-run operation leads a free three-hour bike tour around Paris every Friday night from 10 P.M. The route changes every week, and be sure to rent a bike in advance if you don't have one.

 E2 BEGINS IN FRONT OF THE HÔTEL DE VILLE, 4E
HTTP://MEMBRES.LYCOS.FR/PRV

 **MAP 8 | BASTILLE**

DANCING ON THE SQUARE TINO ROSSI
Open-air dancing beside the Seine takes place in this square every night June–September, with "stages" for tango, salsa, and swing. All ages and abilities are welcome.

MAP 8 E2 ⓐ25 QUAI ST-BERNARD, 5E

PROMENADE PLANTÉE
Stroll from the Gare de Lyon to the Bois de Vincennes through a park constructed atop an ancient train trestle and along paths alive with wild and cultivated vegetation.

MAP 8 C5 ⓐ23 AV. DAUMESNIL, 12E

ROUE LIBRE BIKE RENTAL
The RATP, the Paris public transportation system, created Roue Libre ("free wheel") centers throughout Paris to encourage bike use with rock-bottom rates and well-equipped bikes with baskets and lights. The Bastille location stays open until 1 A.M. on Friday nights.

MAP 8 C2 ⓐ19 37 BD. BOURDON, 4E
01-44-54-19-29 WWW.ROUELIBRE.FR

OVERVIEW MAP

BOATING IN THE BOIS DE VINCENNES
There's nothing more romantic than rowing around the scenic lake of the Bois de Vincennes. Boat rentals are available March–October for up to four adults. Bring a picnic.

OVERVIEW MAP E6 BOIS DE VINCENNES, LAC DAUMESNIL, 12E

CANAL ST-MARTIN
The greening of Paris is most evident along this hip waterway, formerly an industrial path. Its charming locks are brought to life anew by summer picnickers, boutiques, and bars.

OVERVIEW MAP C5 QUAI JEMMAPES AND QUAI DE VALMY, 10E

FAT TIRE BIKE AND CITY SEGWAY TOURS
Enjoy a leisurely day or evening bike tour in English around Paris, or day trips to Versailles and Giverny. Tours are also available on super-cool Segways.

OVERVIEW MAP D2 24 RUE EDGAR FAURE (BTWN. AV. DE SUFFREN AND BD. DE GRENELLE), 15E 01-56-58-10-54
WWW.FATTIREBIKETOURSPARIS.COM OR
WWW.CITYSEGWAYTOURS.COM

THE RIVER REVIVAL

The Paris Plage debuted in 2001, when the mayor turned the choked motorways along the river into sandy beaches with palm trees and chaise longes. Ever since, Parisians have been reveling in the delights of Seine-side entertainment. In addition to the many floating bars and dance clubs now moored along the cobblestoned quais, the city plans to open a permanent floating swimming pool by the Pont Tolbiac (near Bibliothèque Nationale Mitterand in the 13th arrondissement) in late 2006. The pedestrian-only **Passerelle des Arts (p. 5)** hosts picnicking locals from spring through fall and also has the added perk of offering the best sunset views in town.

FRIDAY NIGHT FEVER SKATE

This weekly phenomenon attracts up to 20,000 skaters for about three hours of fast-paced blading. Its is also an amusing spectator sport for less-expert enthusiasts. It starts Friday nights at 10 P.M.

OVERVIEW MAP **D3**   MEET AT TOUR MONTPARNASSE IN FRONT OF THE TRAIN STATION, 14E   WWW.PARI-ROLLER.COM

HORSE RACING AT THE BOIS DE BOULOGNE

Whether it's flat racing or steeplechase that gets your adrenaline going, you've got two racetracks to choose from and free admission to the standing-only *pelouse* (lawn).

OVERVIEW MAP **D1**   BOIS DE BOULOGNE, HIPPODROME DE LONGCHAMP AND HIPPODROME D'AUTEUIL, 16E   01-40-71-47-47

PARC ANDRÉ CITROËN

This contemporary, riverside park replaced a Citroën car factory with imaginative water features and room for up to 15 passengers at a time in a giant, anchored hot-air balloon.

OVERVIEW MAP **D2**   QUAI ANDRÉ CITROËN, 15E

PARC DE BELLEVILLE

Some of the best views of Paris can be seen from this contemporary, hillside park built on top of an old quarry. The cascading fountain is the longest in the city.

OVERVIEW MAP **C5**   RUE COURONNES OR RUE JULIEN LACROIX, 20E

PARC DE BERCY

Drop in for a stroll beneath the century-old trees of this creatively designed contemporary park in Paris's former wine-bottling district next to Bercy Village.

OVERVIEW MAP **E5**   41 RUE PAUL BELMONDO, 12E   01-44-74-09-09

PARC DE BERCY   PARC DE LA VILLETTE

PARC DE LA VILLETTE
This is a vast, contemporary park with a kid-friendly science museum, concert hall, and several whimsical playgrounds such as a giant dragon slide. The vintage merry-go-round and free movies in July and August draw in thousands.

OVERVIEW MAP **B5**   30 AV. CORENTIN CARIOU, 19E
01-40-03-75-75

PARC DES BUTTES CHAUMONT
Ascend to wild nature in this hilltop park created in the 19th century. You can picnic on its grassy lawns – a rarity in the city's manicured parks.

OVERVIEW MAP **B5**   ACCESS VIA RUE MANIN OR RUE BOTZARIS, 19E

PARC MONTSOURIS
Sweeping lawns perfect for sunbathing, 100-year-old trees, and a picturesque lake make this romantic English-style park a popular retreat with locals and university students.

OVERVIEW MAP **E4**   BD. JOURDAN (AT RER CITÉ UNIVERSITAIRE), 14E

PISCINE BUTTE-AUX-CAILLES
These three pools – one indoors and two outdoors – are historically listed, art deco-era structures. Don't forget your bathing cap!

OVERVIEW MAP **E4**   5 PL. PAUL VERLAINE, 13E
01-45-89-60-05

ROLAND GARROS
This stadium plays host to the French Open. Tickets for the Grand Slam event may be hard to come by, but the Tenniseum, a multimedia tennis museum, offers behind-the-scenes tours of the stadium to the public year-round.

OVERVIEW MAP **D1**   2 AV. GORDON BENNETT (NEAR PORTE D'AUTEUIL), 16E
01-47-43-48-48   WWW.FFT.FR/ROLANDGARROS/FR

HOTELS

Most luxurious spa: **FOUR SEASONS GEORGE V,** p. 88

Best bathrooms: **HÔTEL SEZZ,** p. 93

Most romantic: **HÔTEL BOURG TIBOURG,** p. 91

Hippest bar: **HÔTEL PLAZA ATHÉNÉE,** p. 89

Best budget value: **HÔTEL BRITANNIQUE,** p. 90

Most peaceful: **HÔTEL DUC DE ST-SIMON,** p. 88

Most historic atmosphere: **HÔTEL ST-MERRY,** p. 91

PRICE KEY

$ ROOMS UNDER $200

$$ ROOMS $200-300

$$$ ROOMS OVER $300

MAP 1 QUARTIER LATIN/LES ILES

HÔTEL DES GRANDES ECOLES *ROMANTIC* $
This country-style hotel has three buildings around a leafy, private courtyard and 51 rooms decorated in pretty, floral fabrics.

 E5 ⊕21 75 RUE DU CARDINAL LEMOINE, 5E
01-43-26-79-23 WWW.HOTEL-GRANDES-ECOLES.COM

HÔTEL DES GRANDS HOMMES *ROMANTIC* $
Friendly owners and a great location greet guests into this 18th-century building featuring brass beds, exposed beams, and a flower garden.

 F3 ⊕25 17 PL. DU PANTHÉON, 5E
01-46-34-19-60 WWW.HOTELDESGRANDSHOMMES.COM

HÔTEL DU JEU DE PAUME *QUAINT* $$
Retreat on the Ile-St-Louis in this 17th-century tennis court transformed into a well-lit and airy hotel with tiled floors, timbered ceilings, and a spacious garden.

 A5 ⊕6 54 RUE ST-LOUIS-EN-L'ILE, 4E
01-43-26-14-18 WWW.JEUDEPAUMEHOTEL.COM

MAP 2 ST-GERMAIN-DES-PRÉS

L'HÔTEL *CHIC* $$$
The luxuriously hip Jacques Garcia–designed hotel where Oscar Wilde took his last breath takes over-the-top opulence to new heights with an indoor swimming pool and *fumoir* (smoking room).

 B2 ⊕4 13 RUE DES BEAUX ARTS, 6E
01-44-41-99-00 WWW.L-HOTEL.COM

HÔTEL ARTUS *CHIC* $$
Formerly the Buci Latin, Artus is a stylish boutique hotel on a popular market street. Rooms feature flat screen TVs, funky jewel-toned walls, and animal-print fabrics.

 D3 ⊕25 34 RUE DE BUCI, 6E
01-43-29-07-20 WWW.ARTUSHOTEL.COM

HÔTEL BEL-AMI *CHIC* $$
Known for its minimalist chic design, the Bel Ami features rooms in calm pastels or citrus orange, fresh orchids throughout, a fireplace lounge, and a "Wellness Center" opened in 2005.

 D2 ⊕21 7-11 RUE ST-BENOÎT, 6E
01-42-61-53-53 WWW.HOTEL-BEL-AMI.COM

HÔTEL D'ANGLETERRE *QUAINT* $$
Elegantly decorated with period furnishings and high ceilings, most rooms have exposed wooden beams and views of the hotel garden. Hemingway had Room 14 when he first came to Paris.

C2 ⊕9 44 RUE JACOB, 6E
01-42-60-34-72 WWW.HOTEL-DANGLETERRE.COM

HÔTEL DES MARRONNIERS   LA VILLA

HÔTEL DE L'ABBAYE ST-GERMAIN *ROMANTIC* $$

A former convent, l'Abbaye's cobbled courtyard and fireplace lounge lead to well-appointed guest rooms with antique furnishings, designer floral fabrics, and flat-screen TVs.

 F2 ❶42   10 RUE CASSETTE, 6E
01-45-44-38-11 WWW.HOTEL-ABBAYE.COM

HÔTEL DES MARRONNIERS *ROMANTIC* $

Set back from the street by a cobbled courtyard, this adorable hotel has its own private garden shaded by chestnut trees. Rooms are small but quiet, with beautifully coordinated fabrics.

 C2 ❶11   21 RUE JACOB, 6E
01-43-25-30-60 WWW.HOTEL-MARRONNIERS.COM

RELAIS CHRISTINE *CHIC* $$$

This 16th-century convent has kept its medieval feel with rich colors and exposed wooden beams. Rooms are individually decorated in Toile de Jouy and Louis XIII furnishings.

 C4 ❶18   3 RUE CHRISTINE, 6E
01-40-51-60-80 WWW.RELAIS-CHRISTINE.COM

LE RELAIS MEDICIS *ROMANTIC* $

Provence inspired the decor of this charming hotel, with exposed stone walls, painted woodwork, and antique furnishings. Rooms overlook a tranquil patio with a fountain.

 E5 ❶38   23 RUE RACINE, 6E
01-43-26-00-60

RELAIS ST-GERMAIN *QUAINT* $$

This 17th-century building retains its historic mood with period furniture, luxurious fabrics, and antique prints. Each room is named for a different author.

 D5 ❶27   9 CARREFOUR DE L'ODÉON, 6E
01-44-27-07-97

LA VILLA *CHIC* $$

Philippe Starck-designed bathrooms enhance the look of this chic hotel's bold, contemporary rooms, each epitomizing St-Germain style.

 C2 ❶10   29 RUE JACOB, 6E
01-43-26-60-00

MAP 3 INVALIDES

HÔTEL DE L'UNIVERSITÉ *QUAINT* $

Formerly a Benedictine convent, this Left Bank favorite near St-Germain-des-Prés has stone fireplaces, simple antique furnishings, and plenty of space – a rarity in Paris!

MAP 3 B6 **H**12 22 RUE DE L'UNIVERSITÉ, 7E
01-42-61-09-39

HÔTEL DUC DE ST-SIMON *ROMANTIC* $$

This peaceful French country-style retreat has elegantly appointed rooms and gorgeous tiled bathrooms, all set around a shaded central courtyard.

MAP 3 C5 **H**22 14 RUE DE ST-SIMON, 7E
01-44-39-20-20

HÔTEL LUTÉTIA *GRAND* $$$

Built in 1911, this is the only true palace hotel on the Left Bank, with contemporary artworks throughout and a plush jazz bar frequented by chic Parisians.

MAP 3 D6 **H**35 45 BD. RASPAIL, 6E
01-49-54-46-46   WWW.LUTETIA-PARIS.COM

LE MONTALEMBERT *CHIC* $$$

One of the earliest designer boutique hotels in Paris, the Montalembert offers wildly contrasting styles of cool contemporary or cozy classic guest rooms just a few blocks from St-Germain-des-Prés.

MAP 3 B5 **H**10 3 RUE MONTALEMBERT, 7E
01-45-49-68-68

LE WALT *CHIC* $$

This contemporary boutique hotel near the Eiffel Tower features wooden floors, milk chocolate- and plum-colored fabrics, and enormous paintings above each bed.

MAP 3 E2 **H**39 37 AV. DE LA MOTTE PICQUET, 7E
01-45-51-55-83   WWW.INWOODHOTEL.COM/WALT

MAP 4 TOUR EIFFEL/ARC DE TRIOMPHE/TROCADÉRO

FOUR SEASONS GEORGE V *GRAND* $$$

A sumptuous palace hotel dripping with crystal, marble, silk, and antique furnishings, the George V is also renowned for its Versailles-style swimming pool and spa decorated in Toile de Jouy. Le Cinq restaurant features Michelin-starred cuisine and wines chosen by an award-winning sommelier.

MAP 4 B4 **H**17 31 AV. GEORGE V, 8E
01-49-52-70-00   WWW.FOURSEASONS.COM/PARIS

HÔTEL LANCASTER *GRAND* $$$

The Lancaster has long been a favored destination for those seek-

HÔTEL DUC DE ST-SIMON   HÔTEL GEORGE SAND

ing comfortable seclusion. Enjoy the private art collection and
Second Empire antiques.

 7 RUE DE BERRI, 8E
01-40-76-40-76   WWW.HOTEL-LANCASTER.FR

HÔTEL PLAZA ATHÉNÉE *GRAND* *$$$*
A favorite with fashionistas and visiting royalty, this hotel features
opulently grand guest rooms, a stylish contemporary bar, and an
haute-cuisine restaurant run by French superchef Alain Ducasse.

 25 AV. MONTAIGNE, 8E
01-53-67-66-65   WWW.PLAZA-ATHENEE-PARIS.COM

HÔTEL RAPHAEL *GRAND* *$$$*
Favored by U.S. presidents, including Ford and Bush Senior, the
Raphael drips class. Its 90 rooms are crowded with antiques, and
privacy is guaranteed.

 17 AV. KLÉBER, 16E
01-53-64-32-00   WWW.RAPHAEL-HOTEL.COM

MAP 5 GRANDS BOULEVARDS

HÔTEL COSTES *CHIC* *$$$*
Statues of Roman gods hold court in the Costes's garden. The
hotel's sumptuous velvety interior and indoor swimming pool
attract jet-setting models and media types.

 239 RUE ST-HONORÉ, 1ER
01-42-44-50-00   WWW.HOTELCOSTES.COM

HÔTEL DES TUILERIES *QUAINT* *$*
Exceptionally located just off a market street near the Tuileries
Gardens, this 18th-century mansion is decorated with delicate
antiques, gilt-framed paintings, and Persian carpets.

 10 RUE ST-HYACINTHE, 1ER
01-42-61-04-17   WWW.HOTEL-DES-TUILERIES.COM

HÔTEL GEORGE SAND *QUAINT* *$*
This cozy hotel combines crisp and contemporary decor with

HÔTEL BRITANNIQUE   HÔTEL BOURG TIBOURG

historic architectural details right around the corner from the
Opéra Garnier and Parisian department stores.

 A1 **H1** 26 RUE DES MATHURINS, 9E
01-47-42-63-47

HÔTEL MEURICE *GRAND* $$$
Built in 1817, this grande dame of a palace hotel overlooking the
Tuileries is a kaleidoscope of mosaic tiling, marble, and crystal
with enormous guest rooms decked out in Louis XVI furnishings.
Dining options include an elegant Winter Garden tearoom and a
Michelin-starred restaurant.

 E3 **H40** 228 RUE DE RIVOLI, 1ER
01-44-58-10-10 WWW.MEURICEHOTEL.COM

HÔTEL RITZ *GRAND* $$$
Gilded to the hilt with a staff numbering nearly 500, the Ritz will
satisfy your every whim. The health club alone, which resembles a
Roman bathhouse, is worth a visit.

 C3 **H23** 15 PL. VENDÔME, 1ER
01-43-16-30-30 WWW.RITZPARIS.COM

PARK HYATT PARIS-VENDÔME *GRAND* $$$
Sleek mahogany, pale limestone, and rough bronze sculptures
form the backdrop for hi-tech luxuries like Bang & Olufsen TVs and
under-floor heating.

 C3 **H22** 5 RUE DE LA PAIX, 2E
01-58-71-12-34 HTTP://PARIS.VENDOME.HYATT.COM

MAP 6 | LOUVRE/LES HALLES

HÔTEL BRITANNIQUE *ROMANTIC* $
The Britannique retains many of its attractive 19th-century features while also embracing modern facilities, such as Internet
access, in its richly decorated rooms.

 E6 **H40** 20 AV. VICTORIA, 1ER
01-42-33-74-59 WWW.HOTEL-BRITANNIQUE.FR

HÔTEL VICTOIRES OPÉRA   *CHIC $$*
Redone in a tasteful minimalist style, the hotel's greatest charm is
its location – on the bustling market street Montorgueil.

 B4 ❸3   56 RUE MONTORGUEIL, 2E
01-42-36-41-08

RELAIS DU LOUVRE   *QUAINT $*
This typically Parisian hotel overlooking the Louvre Museum
has air-conditioned rooms decorated in colorful floral prints and
exposed wooden beams.

 F3 ❹44   19 RUE DES PRÊTRES ST-GERMAIN L'AUXERROIS, 1ER
01-40-41-96-42   WWW.RELAISDULOUVRE.COM

 MARAIS

HOME PLAZZA BASTILLE   *ROMANTIC $$$*
Every room in this art deco-style hotel overlooks a 4,877-meter
(16,000-foot) flowered courtyard, ensuring a tranquil night's
sleep. A fitness center was added in 2005.

 A6 ❸3   74 RUE AMELOT, 11E
01-40-21-20-00   WWW.HOMEPLAZZA.COM

HÔTEL BOURG TIBOURG   *ROMANTIC $$*
This jewel-box hotel designed by Jacques Garcia features a
voluptuous neo-Byzantine interior of mosaic tiling, exotic scented
candles, and luxurious fabrics in rich colors.

 D3 ❸33   19 RUE DU BOURG-TIBOURG, 4E
01-42-78-47-39

HÔTEL CARON DE BEAUMARCHAIS   *QUAINT $*
Named for the playwright Beaumarchais (*The Marriage of Figaro*),
who lived down the street, this charming hotel has exposed wood-
en beams and period furniture upholstered in fine floral fabrics.

 E4 ❹51   12 RUE VIEILLE DU TEMPLE, 4E
01-42-72-34-12   WWW.CARONDEBEAUMARCHAIS.COM

HÔTEL DU PETIT MOULIN   *CHIC $$*
Each of the 10 rooms in this historically listed building has been
individually decorated by none other than French fashion designer
Christian Lacroix.

 B4 ❸8   29-31 RUE DU POITOU, 3E
01-42-74-10-10   WWW.PARIS-HOTEL-PETITMOULIN.COM

HÔTEL ST-MERRY   *QUAINT $*
A step out of the Middle Ages, this former presbytery of the adjoin-
ing St-Merry Church is filled with authentic Gothic furnishings. The
lack of TVs and an elevator adds to the monkish asceticism.

MAP 7 D1 ❷24   78 RUE DE LA VERRERIE, 4E
01-42-78-14-15

8 BASTILLE

PAVILLON DE LA REINE *ROMANTIC* $$$
Housed in a picture-perfect 17th-century mansion on Place des
Vosges, this hotel's original wooden beams are a beautiful match
for the Louis XIII-style antiques, period tapestries, and fireplaces.
Rooms feature four-poster beds, French windows, and views over
a flowered courtyard.

MAP **8** A1 **H** 1 28 PL. DES VOSGES, 4E
01-40-29-19-19 WWW.PAVILLON-DE-LA-REINE.COM

 9 MONTMARTRE

HÔTEL DES ARTS *QUAINT* $
Soak up the authentic Parisian atmosphere at this quiet
Montmartre location with cheerful, brightly hued rooms and spec-
tacular upper-floor views.

MAP **9** D3 **H** 11 5 RUE THOLOZÉ, 18E
01-46-06-30-52 WWW.ARTS-HOTEL-PARIS.COM

TERRASS HÔTEL *ROMANTIC* $$
One of the grandest hotels in Montmartre, this family-run
hotel features breathtaking views from its upper rooms and a
panoramic rooftop restaurant.

MAP **9** D2 **H** 9 12 RUE JOSEPH DE MAISTRE, 18E
01-44-92-34-14 WWW.TERRASS-HOTEL.COM

VILLA ROYALE *CHIC* $$
With boudoir-style luxury just off the racy Place Pigalle, the villa
steeps its guests in plush comfort with high-tech gadgets like
whirlpool tubs and plasma TV screens.

MAP **9** E4 **H** 26 2 RUE DUPERRÉ, 9E
01-55-31-78-78

OVERVIEW MAP

LE BRISTOL *GRAND* $$$
This 1925 palace boasts Louis XV- and Louis XVI-style luxury
rooms. The magnificent gardens are topped only by the one-of-a-
kind enclosed rooftop pool.

OVERVIEW MAP **C3** 112 RUE DU FAUBOURG ST-HONORÉ, 8E
01-53-43-43-00 WWW.HOTEL-BRISTOL.COM

HÔTEL DANIEL *ROMANTIC* $$$
Daniel is more like a private Parisian home than a hotel, with

HÔTEL DES ARTS   MURANO URBAN RESORT

exotic chinoiserie prints and jewel-toned luxurious fabrics mixed with Middle Eastern furnishings – the antidote to minimalism!

OVERVIEW MAP **C3**   8 RUE FRÉDÉRIC BASTIAT, 8E
01-42-56-17-00   WWW.HOTELDANIELPARIS.COM

HÔTEL SEZZ   *CHIC* $$

The sexy, masculine interior by French furniture designer Christophe Pillet includes camp-style beds in the center of the room and the largest bathtubs in Paris.

OVERVIEW MAP **D2**   6 AV. DU FRÉMIET, 16E
01-56-75-26-26   WWW.HOTELSEZZ.COM

MURANO URBAN RESORT   *CHIC* $$$

Bond wannabes with an Austin Powers streak love this ultra-trendy hotel's fingerprint sensor door locks, adjustable colored lights, and funky pop art decor.

OVERVIEW MAP **C5**   13 BD. DU TEMPLE, 3E
01-42-71-20-00   WWW.MURANORESORT.COM

CITY ESSENTIALS

CHARLES DE GAULLE INTERNATIONAL AIRPORT

Most international flights land at Charles de Gaulle, near the village of Roissy-en-France, which is located 23 kilometers (14 miles) north of the city. To get to Paris, there are several options.

The RER B train takes 45 minutes to central Paris (Chatelet-Les Halles) leaving from Terminal 2. If you arrive at Terminal 1, there is a free shuttle bus to Terminal 2.

Air France buses leave from both terminals every 15 minutes and stop at Porte Maillot and Place Charles de Gaulle (the Arc de Triomphe). The Roissybus runs every 15 minutes 6 A.M.–10:30 P.M. and every 20 minutes after 7 P.M. It will deposit you in central Paris at the Opéra Garnier.

You can also use a door-to-door shuttle service, which caters almost entirely to U.S.-based customers and has an English-speaking staff. Prices are lower with two or more people. One reliable service is Airport Connection (01-43-65-55-55); you can make reservations in advance on their website at www.airport-connection.com.

A taxi takes 30 minutes to an hour, depending on traffic, so it's not necessarily faster. But it is probably the best option if you have a party of three and/or a lot of luggage.

ARRIVING BY TRAIN

Paris has six main train stations, each providing service to different regions. These are: Gare d'Austerlitz (southwest France, Spain, and Portugal), Gare de l'Est (eastern France and Germany), Gare de Lyon (southern France, Switzerland, and Italy), Gare Montparnasse (Brittany), Gare St-Lazare (Normandy), and Gare du Nord (Benelux and London). Two types of trains serve each station: *grandes lignes* (08-91-36-20-20) for long-distance, and *banlieue* (08-92-35-35-39) for suburban lines. The official French train website, www.sncf.com, is notoriously difficult to use. (Train tickets can be purchased painlessly at any of several SNCF boutiques in central Paris.)

Be sure to *composter* (punch) your ticket in one of the little yellow machines in the station before you board the train.

PUBLIC TRANSPORTATION

Paris has an extraordinary system of cheap public transportation. Metro lines link the entire city and run between 5:30 A.M. and about 1 A.M. They are numbered and also identified by final destination (for example, Line 1 westbound is indicated by La Défense; eastbound by Château de Vincennes). The same ticket is used for buses (but they must be punched in the machine next to the driver or by the door). Push the red button to signal that you want to get off (Arrêt Demandé). You can transfer as many times as necessary on the metro using one ticket. To transfer between buses, you have to use a second ticket. If you miss the last metro, you can catch the Noctambus (nightbus), which runs 1–5:30 A.M. nightly, from the Chatelet down the major roads of the city and into the suburbs. A bus on each line is sent out every hour. A metro ticket also allows you to ride on the RER suburban trains within Paris city limits.

TAXIS

Taxis are available throughout Paris and there are taxi stands at major squares. A white light on the rooftop sign indicates that a taxi is free. A smaller yellow light means it is occupied. Taxi charges depend on the time of day and your location: Zone A is central Paris and Zone C takes you to the suburbs. There is a small extra charge for baggage. If you call for a taxi pickup, the fare will be counted from the moment the taxi heads in your direction.

DRIVING AND RENTING A CAR

British, E.U., and U.S. driver's licenses are all valid in France. However, driving in Paris should be kept to a minimum unless you relish the challenges of contending with one-way streets and maniac drivers in congested traffic.

Street parking is metered in central Paris; you buy a ticket from a machine on the sidewalk and place it inside your windshield. There are public garages throughout the city that make the process more manageable, and expensive.

The major international rental companies are all represented in France, as are a range of European firms. It is cheaper to shop around before you leave and, ideally, make car-rental arrangements in advance. The question of insurance should be resolved ahead of time, too. Most major car-rental companies have offices at the airport and in or near central Paris, usually at a train station.

CURRENCY EXCHANGE

France, as a member of the European Union, uses the euro (€) as its standard currency. Not all French banks change money, and their commissions vary. Banks are usually open Monday-Friday 9 A.M.-5 P.M. (some close at lunchtime) and often on Saturday mornings. Most of them will cash travelers checks and some will give cash advances to Visa cardholders.

There are Travelex agencies in each of the two terminals at Charles de Gaulle airport. In addition, Thomas Cook maintains 50 branches in Paris, many of them in train stations. Look for the signs indicating a bureau de change.

AMERICAN EXPRESS
MAP 5 A2 11 RUE SCRIBE, 9E
01-47-14-50-00

THOMAS COOK
MAP 4 A4 52 AV. DES CHAMPS-ELYSÉES, 8E
01-42-89-80-33

EMBASSIES

BRITISH EMBASSY
OVERVIEW MAP C3 35 RUE DE FAUBOURG ST-HONORÉ, 8E
01-44-51-31-00

CANADIAN EMBASSY
MAP 4 B5 35 AV. MONTAIGNE, 8E
01-44-43-29-00

U.S. EMBASSY
OVERVIEW MAP C3 2 AV. GABRIEL, 8E
01-43-12-22-22

U.S. EMBASSY: AMERICAN CITIZEN SERVICES
MAP 5 D2 2 RUE ST-FLORENTIN, 1ER
01-43-12-22-22

VISITOR INFORMATION

The Paris Visitors Bureau, the city's official tourist office, offers help with hotel reservations in French and English, information about exhibitions, free maps and brochures, sight-seeing information, and tour bookings. You can also buy here the Paris City Passport (a booklet of discount coupons), Paris Visite transport passes, and the Paris Museum-Monument Pass. The office is open Monday–Saturday 10 A.M.-7 P.M. and Sunday and public holidays 11 A.M.-7 P.M.

PARIS VISITORS BUREAU
MAP 5 D5 25 RUE DES PYRAMIDES
08-92-68-30-00 WWW.PARISINFO.COM

WEATHER

Paris is wet in spring, sometimes warm and humid, then suddenly chilly. The rain might be a drizzle or a torrential downpour. In winter, snow is rare, temperatures are cold, and skies are dark at 5 P.M. Summer days can be uncomfortably hot but the long evenings compensate. Autumn weather is the most stable of the year.

HOURS

Paris is a late-night city, even an all-night city in places like Bastille, rue Oberkampf, and Champs-Elysées. Otherwise, most restaurants, cafés, and wine bars shut their doors by 1 A.M. In general, Paris shops are open Monday–Saturday 10 A.M.–7 P.M. (some of the larger grocery stores, like Monoprix, are now open until 9 P.M.). Smaller shops and businesses sometimes close at lunch, usually 12:30–2 P.M., and on Mondays. Many family-owned shops and restaurants are closed all or part of August.

FESTIVALS AND EVENTS

MARCH

Salon du Livre: International literary lights descend on Paris for one week for this annual book fair. Mid-March. (Paris Expo, Porte de Versailles, 01-44-41-40-50)

APRIL

Paris Marathon: The race starts at the Place de la Concorde and finishes on avenue Foch. The Champs-Elysées offers the best view. First week of April. (01-41-33-15-68)

MAY

French Open: This prestigious tennis tournament is one of the four Grand Slam events and draws big names. Last week of May/first week of June. (Stade Roland Garros, tickets 08-25-16-75-16)

JUNE

Fête du Cinéma: For three days, film buffs can see as many films as they want in any movie theater in Paris for €1.50 per ticket. End of June.

Fête de la Musique: In Paris, the longest day of the year is also the loudest. Singers of all stripes perform for free in parks and live bands jam in the streets. June 21.

Gay Pride Parade: The annual gay and lesbian parade follows a different route every year, but it's a nonstop party in the Marais. Last Saturday in June.

Garçons du Café: In this race, café waiters and waitresses run around carrying a tray with a bottle and glass, and any breaks mean they're out. Late June. (08-92-68-31-12)

JULY

Bastille Day: The French national holiday is celebrated by an impressive military parade up the Champs-Elysées, fireworks by the Eiffel Tower, and festive balls at certain fire stations. July 14.

Tour de France: Could the world's most famous bicycle race finish anywhere other than Paris? No matter where the three-week and 3,606-kilometer (2,240-mile) race begins, it always ends on the Champs-Elysées. July. (01-41-33-15-00)

SEPTEMBER

Les Journées du Patrimoine (Heritage Days): Some 300 historic sites – mainly fancy government buildings – usually off-limits to the public are open free of charge. Third weekend of September.

OCTOBER

Fête des Vendanges à Montmartre: The only vineyard in Paris produces 500 bottles a year, a phenomenon celebrated with a street festival. First Saturday in October. (Montmartre, 01-42-52-42-00)

NOVEMBER

Illuminations de Noël: The trees along avenue Montaigne and the Champs-Elysées are adorned with white Christmas lights that glitter 5 P.M.–midnight. November 15–January 5.

DISABLED ACCESS

In general, Paris does little to meet the needs of travelers with disabilities. The Paris metro is not accessible; nor are the buses, now with a few exceptions. The intercity rail system (RER lines A, B, C, D, and E) has access in places. Taxis are required by law to take passengers in wheelchairs if they can. Recently constructed and renovated museums and public buildings often have access, but it's best to check ahead of time. Public toilets with disabled access are rare.

SAFETY

As in any city, visitors to Paris should travel smart, stay alert, and take precautionary safety measures. Pickpockets target tourists in train stations and on the metro. Rental cars are often broken into and valuable items should never be left inside. Avoid the Bois du Boulogne, Bois de Vincennes, and the Paris suburbs at night.

HEALTH AND EMERGENCY SERVICES

For immediate emergency services, call 15 for an ambulance (SAMU), 17 for the police, and 18 for the fire department. SOS Médecins (01-47-07-77-77) makes house calls (the fee is only slightly higher than at the office); SOS Dentaire (01-43-37-51-00) provides emergency dental treatment. Pharmacists are also trained in first aid and can arrange a visit to a local doctor or an ambulance.

Don't leave home without travel insurance that includes medical coverage. The standard of health care is high in Paris (lower in public hospitals and lower than U.S. private practice), but non-E.U. citizens are only covered if they have their own insurance.

PHARMACIES

There is a pharmacy – sometimes several – on nearly every block in Paris's downtown.

PHARMACIE DE LA MAIRIE DE PARIS
MAP 7 D3   9 RUE DES ARCHIVES, 4E
01-42-78-53-58

PHARMACIE DE LA SORBONNE
MAP 1 D2   49 RUE DES ECOLES, 5E
01-43-54-26-10

PHARMACIE DES INVALIDES
MAP 3 E2   25 BD. DE LA TOUR MAUBOURG, 7E
01-47-05-43-77

MEDIA AND COMMUNICATIONS

All the phone numbers in this book are listed as they would be dialed within Paris. French telephone numbers have 10 digits. In Paris and the surrounding region (Ile de France), all land-phone numbers begin with 01 and mobile phones begin with 06. Dial 12 for French telephone directory assistance, 3212 for international assistance.

The télécarte can be used in nearly all public telephones. They are sold at tobacco shops, post offices, metro stations, supermarkets, and France Télécom stores. Each card has either 50 or 120 "units," which can be used from any phone booth (*cabine*) for local or international calls. A chip keeps track of the number of units left after each telephone call. There are also prepaid calling cards (with a toll-free number and PIN code) to use from any kind of phone, which is especially useful when the chip-card slot doesn't work on the streets. For GSM-equipped mobile phones, you can also buy a pay-as-you-go chip to use while in France, from any phone store or newspaper shops in airports.

A French post office is known as "La Poste" (also PTT) and identified by a yellow sign. Normal hours are Monday–Friday 8 A.M.-7 P.M., Saturday 8 A.M.-noon. Most have phone booths, photocopiers, fax machines, and outdoor cash machines. In Paris, the central post and sorting office of the Louvre, at 52 rue du Louvre, is open 24 hours a day. All post offices are listed in the phone book under "Poste, La." The standard rate for a letter within France or to another E.U. country is €0.53; a letter to North America costs €0.90.

Paris is divided into 20 arrondissements ("districts") that follow a clockwise spiral from the center. The first (Premier) arrondissement is abbreviated as 1ER; from there they follow on as 2E, 3E (Deuxième, Troisième), and so on. Each arrondissement has a five-digit postal code beginning with 750 and ending with the arrondissement number.

Paris is a great media city and has a wealth of daily newspapers and weekly and monthly magazines in French. The best-known, if not necessarily best English-language publication is the *International Herald Tribune,* now fully owned by *The New York Times.* There are also two free English-language monthlies published for expats – *The Paris Free Voice* and *WYN* (What You Need) – and a biweekly called *FUSAC* – available at anglophone bookstores and pubs.

INTERNET

CAFÉ ORBITAL
MAP 1 F1 13 RUE DE MÉDICIS, 6E
01-43-25-76-77

CYBER CAFÉ LATIN
OVERVIEW MAP D3 35 BIS, RUE DE FLEURUS, 6E
01-42-22-01-18

SMOKING

Parisians smoke in practically all the city's bars, clubs, and restaurants. Nonsmoking sections are few and far between.

RESERVATIONS AND TIPPING

There are enough Michelin stars hovering over Paris restaurants to form a small constellation, and the gastronome's stay will twinkle with opportunity. But be aware of the serious need for reservations at many places. Trendy spots may require a few days to a week of advance notice; you may need to reserve months ahead for the best tables, depending on the season. If it's any consolation, it's usually worth the wait.

All French restaurants and cafés add 15 percent to the bill for service. Leave extra only if you want to; never more than 5 percent of the tab. It's customary to tip taxis by rounding up the fare, again to a maximum 5 percent.

DRY CLEANERS

LAVERIE DU TEMPLE
MAP 7 D3 27 RUE VIEILLE DU TEMPLE, 4E
01-42-78-41-50

PRESSING DU 7E
MAP 4 D2 37 RUE DE LONGCHAMP, 16E
01-45-53-06-38

SOS NET IMPEC BLANC
MAP 2 F3 31 RUE CASSETTE, 6E
01-42-22-34-03

FRENCH PHRASES

Bienvenue à Paris! Despite the unflattering stereotypes you may have heard about Parisians, you'll find that many of them are happy to help you negotiate their city, and most speak at least rudimentary English. That said, however, please note that the friendliness of the locals increases exponentially when you initiate conversations in French. Even if you've never studied a word, just try. It's a clear sign of respect, and it will be appreciated. Politesse is also a must: Begin every interaction with *"Bonjour, monsieur/madame,"* and disperse thank yous *(merci)* liberally.

THE BASICS

ENGLISH	FRENCH	PRONUNCIATION
Good day	**Bonjour**	*bon-zhoor*
Good evening	**Bon soir**	*bon swahr*
Welcome	**Bienvenue**	*bee-an-veh-new*
Excuse me	**Excusez-moi**	*ex-kooh-zay mwah*
Pardon	**Pardon**	*par-dohn*
Sir	**Monsieur**	*muhs-yur*
Madam	**Madame**	*mah-dahm*
Miss	**Mademoiselle**	*mahd-mwah-zehl*
Do you speak English?	**Parlez-vous anglais?**	*parlay-voo ahn-glay*
I don't speak French.	**Je ne parle pas français.**	*zhuh nuh parl pah frahn-say*
How are you? (formal)	**Comment allez-vous?**	*koh-mohn tah-lay voo*
Very well, thank you.	**Très bien, merci.**	*tray bee-an, mehr-see*
How's it going? (informal)	**Ça va?**	*sah vah*
It's going fine.	**Ça va bien.**	*sah vah bee-an*
My name is...	**Je m'appelle...**	*zhuh mah-pehl...*
What's your name?	**Quel est votre nom?**	*kehl ay voh-treh nohm*
Please	**S'il vous plaît**	*seehl voo play*
Thank you	**Merci**	*mehr-see*
You're welcome.	**Je vous en prie.**	*zhuh voo zhan pree*
No problem	**De rien**	*duh ree-an*
I'm sorry	**Desolé**	*dehs-oh-lay*
Goodbye	**Au revoir**	*ohr-vwah*
Yes	**Oui**	*wee*
No	**Non**	*nohn*

GETTING AROUND

How do I get to...?	**Comment puis-je me rendre à...?**	*koh-mohn pwee-zheh muh rahn-druh ah*
Where is...?	**Où est...?**	*ooh ay*
the subway	**le Métro**	*luh may-troh*
the airport	**l'aéroport**	*lehr-oh-pohr*
the train station	**la gare**	*lah gayr*
the train	**le train**	*luh trahn*
the bus stop	**l'arrêt de bus**	*lah-ray duh boos*
the bus	**l'autobus**	*law-toh-boos*
the exit	**la sortie**	*lah sohr-tee*
the street	**la rue**	*lah roo*
the garden	**le jardin**	*luh zhar-dan*
a taxicab	**un taxi**	*uhn tak-see*
a hotel	**un hôtel**	*uhn oh-tehl*
a toilet	**une toilette**	*oohn twah-let*
a pharmacy	**une pharmacie**	*oohn far-mah-see*
a bank	**une banque**	*oohn bahnk*
a tourist office	**un bureau de tourisme**	*uhn byuh-roh duh tohr-ees-muh*
a telephone	**un téléphone**	*uhn teh-lay-fohn*

HEALTH AND EMERGENCY

Help!	**Au secours!**	*oh she-coor*
I am sick.	**Je suis malade.**	*zhuh swee mah-lahd*
I am hurt.	**Je suis blessé.**	*zhuh swee bleh-say*
I need...	**J'ai besoin de...**	*zhay buh-zwahn duh*
the hospital	**l'hôpital**	*loh-pee-tal*
the doctor	**le médicin**	*luh mayd-san*
an ambulance	**une ambulance**	*oohn am-bew-lahns*
the police	**la police**	*lah poh-lees*
medicine	**médicament**	*meh-dee-kah-mohn*

EATING

I would like...	**Je voudrais...**	*zhuh voo-dray*
a table for two	**une table pour deux**	*oohn tah-bluh poor duh*
the menu	**la carte**	*lah kahrt*
breakfast	**petit déjeuner**	*puh-tee day-zhuh-nay*
lunch	**déjeuner**	*day-zhuh-nay*
dinner	**dîner**	*dee-nay*

the bill	**l'addition**	*lah-dee-syon*
non-smoking	**non fumeur**	*nohn foo-muhr*
a drink	**une boisson**	*oohn bwah-sohn*
a glass of...	**une verre de...**	*oohn vehr duh*
water	**l'eau**	*low*
beer	**bière**	*bee-ehr*
wine	**vin**	*van*
I am...	**Je suis...**	*zhuh swee*
a vegetarian (male)	**végétarien**	*vay-zhay-teh-ree-yan*
a vegetarian (female)	**végétarienne**	*vay-zhay-teh-ree-yehn*
diabetic	**diabétique**	*dee-ah-bay-teek*
allergic	**allergique**	*ah-layr-zheek*
kosher	**kascher**	*kah-shehr*

SHOPPING

Do you have...?	**Avez-vous...?**	*ah-vay-voo*
Where can I buy...?	**Où puis-je acheter...?**	*ooh pwee-zhuh ash-tay*
May I try this?	**Peux-je l'essayer?**	*puh-zhuh leh-say-ay*
How much is this?	**Combien?**	*kohm-bee-an*
cash	**argent**	*ahr-zhahn*
credit card	**carte de crédit**	*kart duh kray-dee*
Too...	**Trop...**	*troh*
small	**petit**	*puh-tee*
large	**grand**	*grahn*
expensive	**cher**	*shehr*

TIME

What time is it?	**Quelle heure est-il?**	*kehl uhr ay teel*
It is...	**Il est...**	*eel ay*
eight o'clock	**huit heures**	*weet uhr*
half past 10	**dix heures et demi**	*deez uhr ay duh-mee*
quarter to five	**cinq heures moins quart**	*sank uhr mwahn kahr*
noon	**midi**	*mee-dee*
midnight	**minuit**	*meen-wee*
during the day	**pendant la journée**	*pehn-dahn lah zhur-nay*
in the morning	**le matin**	*luh mah-tan*
in the afternoon	**l'après-midi**	*lah-pray-mee-dee*
in the evening	**le soir**	*luh swahr*
at night	**la nuit**	*lah nwee*

DAYS OF THE WEEK

Monday	**lundi**	*luhn-dee*
Tuesday	**mardi**	*mahr-dee*
Wednesday	**mercredi**	*mehr-kreh-dee*
Thursday	**jeudi**	*zhuh-dee*
Friday	**vendredi**	*vohn-druh-dee*
Saturday	**samedi**	*sahm-dee*
Sunday	**dimanche**	*dee-mansh*
this week	**cette semaine**	*sett suh-mehn*
this weekend	**ce weekend**	*suh week-end*
today	**aujourd'hui**	*oh-zhor-dwee*
tomorrow	**demain**	*duh-mah*
yesterday	**hier**	*ee-yayr*

MONTHS

January	**janvier**	*zhahn-vee-yay*
February	**février**	*fehv-ree-yay*
March	**mars**	*mars*
April	**avril**	*ahv-reel*
May	**mai**	*may*
June	**juin**	*zhwan*
July	**juillet**	*zhwee-yay*
August	**août**	*oot*
September	**septembre**	*sep-tahm-bruh*
October	**octobre**	*ohk-toh-bruh*
November	**novembre**	*noh-vahm-bruh*
December	**décembre**	*day-cehm-bruh*
this month	**ce mois**	*suh mwah*
this year	**cette année**	*seht ah-nay*
winter	**hiver**	*ee-vehr*
spring	**printemps**	*prehn-tahn*
summer	**été**	*ay-tay*
fall	**automne**	*oh-tuhn*

NUMBERS

zero	**zéro**	*zeh-roh*
one	**un**	*uhn*
two	**deux**	*duh*
three	**trois**	*twah*
four	**quatre**	*kah-truh*
five	**cinq**	*sank*
six	**six**	*sees*
seven	**sept**	*set*
eight	**huit**	*weet*

nine	**neuf**	*nuhf*
10	**dix**	*deez*
11	**onze**	*ohnz*
12	**douze**	*dooz*
13	**treize**	*trehz*
14	**quatorze**	*kah-torz*
15	**quinze**	*kanz*
16	**seize**	*sehz*
17	**dix-sept**	*deez-set*
18	**dix-huit**	*deez-weet*
19	**dix-neuf**	*deez-nuhf*
20	**vingt**	*vanh*
100	**cent**	*sahn*
1,000	**mille**	*meel*

Note: *J* sounds (spelled in the pronunciation key as *zh*) are pronounced like the s in "treasure."

STREET INDEX

Abbreviations Key

Av.: Avenue
Bd.: Boulevard
Carref.: Carrefour
Cr.: Cour
Imp.: Impasse
Pass.: Passage
Pl.: Place
Q.: Quai
R.: Rue
Sq.: Square
V.: Villa

A

Abbaye, Rue de l': Map 2 D3
Abbesses, Pl. des: Map 9 D4
Abbesses, Rue des: Map 9 D3
Abel, Rue: Map 8 D5
Aboukir, Rue d': Map 6 A3
Abreuvoir, Rue de l': Map 9 B3
Acollas, Av. E: Map 3 F1
Agnes, Quai Adrien: Overview Map A5
Albert, Rue Paul: Map 9 B5
Albert Premier de Monaco, Av.: Map 4 E3
Alboni, Sq. de l': Map 4 F2
Alésia, Rue d': Overview Map E3
Alexandre III, Pont: Map 3 B2
Alger, Rue d': Map 5 D4
Aligre, Rue d': Map 8 B6
Allent, Rue: Map 3 B6
Alma, Cité de l': Map 4 D5
Alma, Pl. de l': Map 4 C4
Alma, Pont de l': Map 4 C4
Amélie, Rue: Map 3 D1; Map 4 D6
Amelot, Rue: Map 7 A6; Map 8 A2
Ancienne Comédie, Rue de l': Map 2 C4
Ancre, Pass. de l': Map 6 A6; Map 7 B1
Anglais, Rue des: Map 1 C3
Anjou, Quai d': Map 1 A6; Map 7 F5

Antin, Imp. d': Map 4 B5
Antin, Rue d': Map 5 B4
Antoine, Rue André: Map 9 D4, E4
Anvers, Pl. d': Map 9 D6
Arago, Bd.: Overview Map E4
Aragon, Allée Louis: Map 6 D3
Arbre Sec, Rue de l': Map 6 E4
Archevêché, Pont de l': Map 1 B4
Archevêché, Quai de l': Map 1 B4
Archives, Rue des: Map 7 A3
Arcole, Pont d': Map 1 A3; Map 7 F2
Arcole, Rue d': Map 1 A3; Map 7 F2
Arènes, Rue des: Map 1 E6
Argenteuil, Rue d': Map 5 D5
Argentin, Rue d': Map 4 A1
Argout, Rue d': Map 6 B3
Armée d'Orient, Rue de l': Map 9 C2
Arquebusiers, Rue des: Map 7 B6
Arras, Rue d': Map 1 D5
Arsenal, Rue de l': Map 8 C2
Arts, Passerelle des: Map 2 A2
Asnières, Porte d': Overview Map B2
Assomption, Rue de l': Overview Map D1
Auber, Rue: Map 5 A2
Aubervilliers Porte d': Overview Map A5
Aubigné, Rue Agrippa d': Map 8 D2
Aubriot, Rue: Map 7 D3
Aubry le Boucher, Rue: Map 6 D6; Map 7 D1
Audran, Rue: Map 9 D3
Audubon, Rue: Map 8 D4
Augereau, Rue: Map 4 E6

Auriol, Bd. Vincent: Overview Map E5
Austerlitz, Quai d': Map 8 E5
Austerlitz, Rue d': Map 8 D4
Auteuil, Porte d': Overview Map D1
Ave Maria, Rue de l': Map 7 F5
Azaïs, Rue: Map 9 C5

B

Babylone, Rue de: Map 3 D5
Bac, Rue du: Map 3 D5
Bachaumont, Rue: Map 6 B3
Bachelet, Rue: Map 9 A5
Bagnolet, Porte de: Overview Map C6
Baillet, Rue: Map 6 E4
Bailleul, Rue: Map 6 E3
Bailly, Rue: Map 7 A2
Baltard, Rue: Map 6 D4
Balzac, Rue: Map 4 A3
Banque, Rue de la: Map 5 A6; Map 6 B1
Barbet de Jouy, Rue: Map 3 D4
Barbette, Rue: Map 7 C4
Barbusse, Rue Henri: Overview Map A6
Barres, Rue des: Map 7 E3
Barrier, Imp.: Map 8 B6
Barsacq, Rue André: Map 9 C5
Basfour, Pass.: Map 6 A4
Bassano, Rue de: Map 4 B3
Bastille, Bd. de la: Map 8 C3
Bastille, Pl. de la: Map 8 B3
Bastille, Rue de la: Map 8 B2
Batignolles, Bd. des: Overview Map B3
Bauchart, Rue Quentin: Map 4 A3
Baudelaire, Rue Charles: Map 8 B5
Baudin, Rue Alphonse: Map 7 A6

Breton, Allée André: Map 6 D4

Bretonvilliers, Rue de: Map 1 A6

Briand, Av. Aristide: Overview Map F3

Brignole, Rue: Map 4 C3

Briquet, Pass.: Map 9 D6

Briquet, Rue: Map 9 D6

Brissac, Rue de: Map 8 D2

Brosse, Rue de: Map 7 E3

Brouardel, Av. du Dr.: Map 4 F5

Bruant, Rue Aristide: Map 9 D3

Brulon, Pass: Map 8 B6

Brune, Bd.: Overview Map E3

Bruxelles, Rue de: Map 9 E2, F1

Bûcherie, Rue de la: Map 1 B2, C3

Buci, Rue de: Map 2 C4

Budé, Rue: Map 1 A5

Buenos Aires, Rue de: Map 4 F4

Buffon, Rue: Overview Map D4; Map 8 F3

Burq, Rue: Map 9 D3

Byron, Rue Lord: Map 4 A3

C

Cadran, Imp. du: Map 9 C6

Caffarelli, Rue: Map 7 A4

Calais, Rue de: Map 9 F2

Callot, Rue Jacques: Map 2 C3

Cambon, Rue: Map 5 C2

Camoëns, Av. de: Map 4 F2

Canada, Pl. du: Map 3 B1; Map 4 B6

Candie, Rue de: Map 8 A5

Canettes, Rue des: Map 2 E3

Canivet, Rue: Map 2 F4

Cantal, Cour du: Map 8 A3

Capron, Rue: Map 9 E1

Capucines, Bd. des: Map 5 A4

Capucines, Rue des: Map 5 C3

Cardinale, Rue: Map 2 C3

Carmes, Rue des: Map 1 D3

Carnot, Av.: Map 4 A1

Carrée, Cour: Map 6 F2

Carrière, Rue Eugène: Map 9 B1

Carriès, Rue Jean: Map 3 F1

Carrousel, Pl. du: Map 5 E6; Map 6 F1

Carrousel, Pont du: Map 2 A1; Map 3 A6 ; Map 5 F6

Casanova, Av. Danielle: Overview Map F5

Casanova, Rue Danielle: Map 5 C4

Cases, Rue Las: Map 3 B4

Cassette, Rue: Map 2 F2

Cassin, Pl. René: Map 6 D4

Castelar, Rue Émilio: Map 8 C5

Castellane, Rue de: Map 5 B1

Castex, Rue: Map 8 B2

Castiglione, Rue de: Map 5 D3

Cauchois, Rue: Map 9 D2

Caulaincourt, Rue: Map 9 A3, D2

Caumartin, Rue de: Map 5 B2

Cavallotti, Rue: Map 9 E1

Célestins, Quai des: Map 7 F5; Map 8 C1

Cendrars, Allée Blaise: Map 6 D4

Cerisaie, Rue de la: Map 8 C2

Cerisole, Rue de: Map 4 B4

César, Rue Jules: Map 8 C4

Chabanais, Rue: Map 5 B5

Chaillot, Rue de: Map 4 B2

Chaillot, Sq. de: Map 4 B3

Chaise, Rue de la: Map 3 C6

Chalgrin, Rue: Map 4 A1

Chalon, Cour de: Map 8 D6

Chalon, Rue de: Map 8 D6

Chambiges, Rue: Map 4 B4

Champ de Mars, Rue du: Map 3 E1; Map 4 E6

Champerret, Porte de: Overview Map B2

Championnet, Rue: Overview Map B4

Champollion, Rue: Map 1 E2

Champs, Galerie des: Map 4 A4

Champs-Elysées, Av. des: Overview Map C3; Map 4 A4

Chanaleilles, Rue de: Map 3 D4

Change, Pont Au: Map 1 A1; Map 7 F1

Chanoinesse, Rue: Map 1 A3

Chantier, Pass du: Map 8 B4

Chantiers: Map 1 C6

Chantres, Rue: Map 1 A3

Chapelle, Bd. de la: Overview Map B4

Chapelle, Porte de la: Overview Map A4

Chapon, Rue: Map 6 A6; Map 7 B2

Chappe, Rue: Map 9 C5

Chaptal, Cité: Map 9 F3

Chaptal, Rue: Map 9 F4

Chardin, Rue: Map 4 F3

Charenton, Porte de: Overview Map A6

Charenton, Rue de: Map 8 B4, C6

Charlemagne, Rue: Map 7 E5

Charles V, Rue: Map 7 E6; Map 8 C1

Charlot, Rue: Map 7 A4

Charonne, Rue de: Map 8 A4

Charron, Rue Pierre: Map 4 A4

Chasles, Rue Michel: Map 8 D5

Châtelet, Pl. du: Map 6 F6; Map 7 E1

Châtillon, Porte de: Overview Map A3

Chaussée d'Antin, Rue de la: Map 5 A3

Chauveau Lagarde, Rue: Map 5 C1

Grauwin, Rue Jean Bouton: Map 8 D6

Gravelle, Av. de: Overview Map E6

Gravilliers, Rue des: Map 6 A6; Map 7 B2

Gréard, Av. Octave: Map 4 F4

Greffulhe, Rue: Map 5 B1

Grégoire de Tours, Rue: Map 2 D4

Grégoire, Rue de l'Abbé: Map 3 E6

Grenelle, Bd. de: Overview Map D2

Grenelle, Rue de: Map 2 E1; Map 3 C4, D2 ; Map 4 D6

Greneta, Cour: Map 6 A5

Greneta, Rue: Map 6 A6, B5; Map 7 A1

Grenier St-Lazare, Rue du: Map 7 B1

Grenier-sur-l'Eau, Rue du: Map 7 E4

Grétry, Rue: Map 5 A5

Greuze, Rue: Map 4 E1

Gribeauval, Rue de: Map 3 B5

Gridaine, Rue Cunin: Map 6 A6; Map 7 A1

Gros Caillou, Rue de: Map 4 E6

Guelma, Villa de: Map 9 E4

Guéménéee, Imp.: Map 8 B2

Guénégaud, Rue: Map 2 B4

Guillaumot, Rue: Map 8 D6

Guillemites, Rue: Map 7 D3

Guisarde, Rue: Map 2 B4

Gustave V de Suède, Av.: Map 4 E3

Guynemer, Rue: Overview Map E1

H

Halévy, Rue: Map 5 A3

Halles, Rue des: Map 6 E5

Hamelin, Rue: Map 4 C2

Hanovre, Rue de: Map 5 A3

Haret, Rue Pierre: Map 9 E2

Harispe du Mal, Rue: Map 4 E5

Harlay, Rue de: Map 2 A5

Harpe, Rue de la: Map 1 C1; Map 2 C6

Haudriettes, Rue des: Map 7 B3

Haussmann, Bd.: Overview Map C3; Map 5 A2

Hautefeuille, Rue: Map 1 C1; Map 2 D6

Hautpavé, Rue: Map 1 C3

Henri IV, Bd.: Map 1 B6; Map 7 F6 ; Map 8 C2

Henri IV, Quai: Map 7 F6; Map 8 D2

Herold, Rue: Map 6 C2

Hirondelle, Rue de l': Map 2 B5

Hoche, Av.: Overview Map C2; Map 4 A2

Homme, Pass. l': Map 8 A4

Hôpital, Bd. de l': Overview Map E4; Map 8 F3

Horloge, Quai de l': Map 1 A1; Map 2 B2 ; Map 6 F6

Hospitalières St-Gervais, Rue des: Map 7 D4

Hôtel Colbert, Rue Del': Map 1 C3

Hôtel de Ville, Pl. de l': Map 7 E2

Hôtel de Ville, Quai de l': Map 7 F3

Hôtel de Ville, Rue de l': Map 7 F4

Houdon, Rue: Map 9 E4

Huchette, Rue de la: Map 1 B2

Hugo, Av. Victor: Overview Map A5, C2; Map 4 B1

Hugo, Bd. Victor: Overview Map A3, B2

Hugo, Pl. Victor: Map 4 C1

Hugo, Rue Victor: Overview Map B2, F5

Hussein Premier de Jordanie, Av.: Map 4 E2

I

Iéna, Av. d': Map 4 C3

Iéna, Pl. d': Map 4 D3

Iéna, Pont d': Map 4 E3

Innocents, Rue des: Map 6 D5

Institut, Pl. de l': Map 2 B2

Invalides, Bd. des: Map 3 D3; Map 3 F4

Invalides, Pl. des: Map 3 C2

Invalides, Pont des: Map 3 B1; Map 4 C6

Italie, Porte d': Overview Map F4

Italiens, Bd. des: Map 5 A4

Ivry, Porte d': Overview Map F5

JK

Jacob, Rue: Map 2 C2

Jardinet, Rue du: Map 2 C5

Jardins St-Paul, Rue des: Map 7 E5

Jarente, Rue de: Map 7 D5

Jaurès, Av. Jean: Overview Map A6, B5

Joffre, Pl.: Map 3 F1; Map 4 F6

Josset, Pass: Map 8 A4

Jour, Rue du: Map 6 C4

Jourdan, Bd.: Overview Map E4

Jouy, Rue de: Map 7 E4

Junot, Av.: Map 9 C3

Jussienne, Rue de la: Map 6 B3

Jussieu, Rue: Map 1 D6; Map 8 F1

Karman, Rue André: Overview Map A5

Keller, Rue: Map 8 A4

Kellermann, Bd.: Overview Map E4

Kepler, Rue: Map 4 B3

Kléber, Av.: Map 4 D2

Kléber, Imp.: Map 4 B2

L

La Boétie, Rue: Map 4 A4

Lacépède, Rue: Map 1 F6

Lacuée, Rue: Map 8 C3

La Forge, Rue Anatole de: Map 4 A1

Périphérique, Bd.: Overview Map A5, D6, E3

Perle, Rue de la: Map 7 C4

Pernelle, Rue: Map 6 E6; Map 7 E1

Pérouse, Rue la: Map 4 C2

Perrault, Rue: Map 6 E3

Perronet, Rue: Map 2 D1; Map 3 B6

Petit Musc, Rue du: Map 7 E6; Map 8 C1

Petit Pont: Map 1 B2

Petit Pont, Rue du: Map 1 B2

Petits Carreaux, Rue des: Map 6 A4

Petits Champs, Rue des: Overview Map C4; Map 5 C5 ; Map 6 C1

Pétrarque, Rue: Map 4 F1

Pétrarque, Sq.: Map 4 F1

Picard, Rue Pierre: Map 9 C6

Picardie, Rue: Map 7 A4

Piémontési, Rue: Map 9 D4

Pierre Premier de Serbie, Av.: Map 4 C3

Pigalle, Pl.: Map 9 E4

Pigalle, Rue Jean Baptiste: Map 9 F4

Pilon, Cité Germain: Map 9 E4

Pilon, Rue Germain: Map 9 D3

Plaine, Porte de la: Overview Map E2

Planche, Rue de la: Map 3 D5

Planquette, Rue Robert: Map 9 D3

Plat d'Etai, Rue du: Map 6 E5

Platanes, Villa des: Map 9 E3

Plâtre, Rue du: Map 7 D2

Poincaré, Av. Raymond: Map 4 D1

Point Show, Galerie: Map 4 A4

Poissoniére, Bd.: Overview Map C4

Poissy, Rue de: Map 1 C5

Poitevins, Rue des: Map 1 C1; Map 2 C6

Poitiers, Rue de: Map 3 B5

Poitou, Rue de: Map 7 B4

Pompidou, Pl. Georges: Map 6 C6; Map 7 D1

Pompidou, Voie Georges: Map 6 F5; Map 7 F4

Poniatowski, Bd.: Overview Map E6

Pont Aux Choux, Rue du: Map 7 A5

Pont de Lodï, Rue du: Map 2 B4

Pont Louis Philippe, Rue du: Map 7 F2

Pont Neuf, Pl. du: Map 2 A4

Pont Neuf, Rue du: Map 6 E4

Pontoise, Rue de: Map 1 C4

Portefoin, Rue de: Map 7 A3

Port Mahon, Rue de: Map 5 B4

Port Royal, Bd.: Overview Map E4

Portugais, Av. des: Map 4 B2

Poulbot, Rue: Map 9 C4

Poulet, Rue: Map 9 A6

Poulletier, Rue: Map 1 A6

Pouvillon, Av. Émile: Map 4 E5

Prague, Rue de: Map 8 B5

Pré Aux Clercs, Rue du: Map 2 D1; Map 3 B6

Prêcheurs, Rue des: Map 6 C5

Pré St-Gervais, Porte du: Overview Map B6

Presbourg, Rue de: Map 4 A2

Prêtres St-Germain l'Auxerrois, Rue des: Map 6 F3

Prêtres St-Séverin, Rue des: Map 1 C2

Prévôt, Rue du: Map 7 E5

Princesse, Rue de: Map 2 E3

Privas, Rue Xavier: Map 1 C2

Prouvaire, Rue des: Map 6 D4

Provence, Rue de: Map 5 A1

Prudhomme, Av. Sully: Map 3 C1; Map 4 C6

Psichari, Rue Ernest: Map 3 D2

Puget, Rue: Map 9 E3

Pyramides, Rue des: Map 5 D5

Quatre Fils, Rue des: Map 7 C4

Quatre Septembre, Rue du: Map 5 A5

Quatre Vents, Rue des: Map 2 D4

Quellard, Cour: Map 8 A4

Quincampoix, Rue: Map 6 C6; Map 7 C1

R

Rachel, Av.: Map 9 E2

Racine, Rue: Map 1 D1; Map 2 D6

Rambuteau, Rue: Map 6 C5; Map 7 C2

Rameau, Rue: Map 5 B5

Ramey, Rue: Map 9 A6

Rapée, Quai de la: Overview Map D5; Map 8 E5

Rapp, Av.: Map 4 E5

Rapp, Sq.: Map 4 E5

Raspail, Bd.: Overview Map D3; Map 3 D6

Réaumur, Rue: Overview Map C4; Map 6 A4 ; Map 7 A2

Récamier, Rue: Map 2 F1; Map 3 C6

Reclus, Av. Elisée: Map 4 E5

Refuzniks, Allée des: Map 4 F4

Régis, Rue: Map 3 E6

Regrattier, Rue le: Map 1 A5

Reine, Cours de la: Map 3 A2

Renaissance, Rue de la: Map 4 B4

Renard, Rue du: Map 7 E2

Rennes, Rue de: Map 2 E2

République, Av. de la: Overview Map C5

Résistance, Pl. de la: Map 4 D5

Reynaud, Rue Léonce: Map 4 C4

Reynie, Rue de la: Map 6 D6; Map 7 D1

St-Sulpice, Rue: Map 2 D4

St-Victor, Rue: Map 1 D5

St-Vincent, Rue: Map 9 B4

Ste-Anastase, Rue: Map 7 B5

Ste-Anne, Rue: Map 5 C5

Ste-Avoie, Pass.: Map 7 C3

Ste-Croix de la Bretonnerie, Rue: Map 7 D3

Ste-Croix de la Brettonerie, Sq.: Map 7 D2

Saintonge, Rue de: Map 7 A4

Sts-Pères, Rue des: Map 2 E1; Map 3 C6

Salembrière, Imp.: Map 1 C2

Sandrié, Imp.: Map 5 A2

Sarrazin, Rue Pierre: Map 1 D1; Map 2 D6

Sarte, Rue André Del: Map 9 B6

Saules, Rue des: Map 9 B3

Sauton, Rue F: Map 1 C3

Sauval, Rue: Map 6 D3

Savoie, Rue de: Map 2 B5

Savorgnan de Brazza, Rue: Map 3 E1; Map 4 F6

Saxe, Av. de: Map 3 F3

Saxe, Villa de: Map 3 F3

Say, Rue: Map 9 E6

Scheffer, Rue: Map 4 F1

Schlœsing, Rue du Commandant S: Map 4 E2

Schomberg, Rue de: Map 8 D2

Schuman, Av. Robert: Map 3 C1; Map 4 C6

Scribe, Rue: Map 5 B3

Sébastopol, Bd. de: Map 6 E6; Map 7 E1

Sedaine, Rue: Map 8 A3

Sédillot, Rue: Map 4 E5

Sédillot, Sq.: Map 4 E5

Séguier, Rue: Map 2 B5

Ségur, Av. de: Map 3 E3

Ségur, Villa: Map 3 F3

Seine, Rue de: Map 2 C3

Selves, Av.: Map 4 A6

Sentier, Rue du: Map 6 A3

Serpente, Rue: Map 1 C1; Map 2 C6

Servandoni, Rue: Map 2 F4

Seveste, Rue: Map 9 C6

Sévigné, Rue de: Map 7 D5

Sèvres, Porte de: Overview Map E2

Sèvres, Rue de: Map 2 F1; Map 3 E5

Sevrien, Galerie le: Map 3 E6

Sèze, Rue de: Map 5 B2

Sizeranne, Rue Maurice de la: Map 3 F4

Soleil, Autoroute du: Overview Map F4

Solférino, Passerelle: Map 3 A4; Map 5 F3

Solférino, Rue de: Map 3 B4

Sommerard, Rue du: Map 1 D3

Sorbonne, Rue de la: Map 1 E2

Soufflot, Rue: Map 1 F3

Soult, Bd.: Overview Map E6

Sourdière, Rue de la: Map 5 D4

Sourdis, Ruelle: Map 7 B3

Spuller, Rue Eugène: Map 7 A3

Steinkerque, Rue de: Map 9 D6

Steinlen, Rue: Map 9 C1

Stevens, Rue Alfred: Map 9 E5

Stravinsky, Pl. Igor: Map 7 D2

Stuart, Rue Marie: Map 6 B4

Suffren, Av. de: Overview Map D3; Map 3 F1; Map 4 F4

Suger, Rue: Map 2 C5

Sully, Pont de: Map 1 B6; Map 7 F6

Sully, Rue de: Map 8 D2

Surcouf, Rue: Map 3 C1; Map 4 C6

TU

Tacherie, Rue de la: Map 7 E2

Taillandiers, Pass. des: Map 8 A4

Talleyrand, Rue de: Map 3 C3

Tardieu, Pl. André: Map 3 E4

Tardieu, Rue: Map 9 C5

Tasse, Rue le: Map 4 F2

Temple, Rue du: Map 7 B3

Tertre, Pl. du: Map 9 C4

Thénard, Rue: Map 1 D3

Thérèse, Rue: Map 5 C5

Thiéré, Pass.: Map 8 A4

Tholozé, Rue: Map 9 D3

Thierry, Allée Thomy: Map 4 F5

Thorez, Av. Maurice: Overview Map F5

Thorigny, Rue de: Map 7 B5

Thouin, Rue: Map 1 F5

Tilsitt, Rue de: Map 4 A2

Tiquetonne, Rue: Map 6 B5

Tiron, Rue: Map 7 E4

Tolbiac, Rue de: Overview Map E5

Toullier, Rue: Map 1 F2

Tour, Rue de la: Map 4 F2

Tour d'Auvergne, Rue de la: Map 9 F6

Tourlaque, Rue: Map 9 C1

Tour Maubourg, Bd. de la: Map 3 D2

Tour Maubourg, Sq. de la: Map 3 D2

Tournefort, Rue: Map 1 F5

Tournelle, Pont de la: Map 1 B5

Tournelle, Quai de la: Map 1 B5

Tournelles, Rue des: Map 7 C6; Map 8 B2

Tournon, Rue de: Map 2 E5

TRANSIT INDEX

INDEX

RESTAURANTS INDEX

NIGHTLIFE INDEX

SHOPS INDEX

HOTELS INDEX

CONTRIBUTORS TO THE THIRD EDITION

REBECCA PERRY MAGNIANT *Shops, Museums and Galleries, Performing Arts*
Rebecca Perry Magniant is an American living in Paris. With her custom shopping tour service, chicshoppingparis.com, she helps visitors discover the secrets of shopping in Paris. She also is a freelance writer whose articles have appeared in *France Today* magazine, among others.

HEATHER STIMMLER-HALL *Introduction, A Day in Paris, Neighborhoods, Sights, Recreation, Hotels*
Heather Stimmler-Hall is an American freelance writer and tour guide who has been living in France since 1995. She specializes in Paris hotels and recreation and contributes regularly to magazines, newspapers, and guidebooks in the United States, United Kingdom, and France. She has been writing about lesser-known aspects of the city in her free monthly newsletter, *Secrets of Paris* (www.secretsofparis.com), since 2001.

OTHER CONTRIBUTORS
Anthony Grant (Restaurants, Nightlife, City Essentials)

CONTRIBUTORS TO PREVIOUS EDITIONS
Mike Gerrard, Alan Brent Gregston, M. K. Hoffman, Mia Lipman, Helen Sillett

PHOTO CREDITS:

© Susannah Sayler: page III, Le Café Thoumieux, Barthelemy, Hôtel Duc de St-Simon; page IX, Tour Eiffel; page X, Notre-Dame, Tour Eiffel, Sacre-Coeur Basilica; page XIV, Jardin des Plantes; Map 1, Notre-Dame, Hôtel du Jeu de Paume; Map 2, Jardin du Luxembourg, Seine Booksellers; Map 3, Pont Alexandre III, Le Café Thoumieux; Map 5, Maître Parfumeur et Gantier; Map 6, Louvre; Map 8, Marché Bastille; Map 9, L'Éte en Pente Douce; page 1, Tour Eiffel; page 5, Jardin du Luxembourg; page 7, Les Invalides; page 10, Jardin de Tuilleries; page 15, Jardin des Plantes; page 17, Sacre-Coeur Basilica; page 19, L'Éte en Pente Douce; page 25, L'Affriolé; page 33, Le Zimmer; Dome du Marais; page 37, L'Éte en Pente Douce; page 39, Le Café Thoumieux; page 43, Le Café Thoumieux; page 49, Hediard, Barthelemy; page 51, Fabrice; page 53, Village Voice, Barthelemy; page 54, Hediard; page 56, Hermès, La Maison du Chocolat, Maître Parfumeur et Gantier; page 61, Bensimon Autour du Monde, Boutique Paris Musées; page 63, Des Petits Hauts, Marché Bastille; page 68, Palais de Tokyo; page 71, Musée de la Magie; page 80, MK2 Bibliothèque; page 84, Parc de Bercy, Parc de la Villette; page 85, Hôtel George Sand, Hôtel Duc de St-Simon; page 87, Hôtel des Marronniers, La Villa; page 89, Hôtel Duc de St-Simon, Hôtel George Sand; page 90, Hôtel Britannique, Hôtel Bourg Tibourg; page 93, Hôtel des Arts, Murano Urban Resort.

Courtesy of L'Artisan Parfumeur: Map 6, page 59

© Gianni Dagli Orti/CORBIS: Mona Lisa, Map 6

Courtesy of LE CAB, page 43

Courtesy of Favela Chic, page 47

Courtesy of Colette, page 54

© Christian des Brosses/Dalí Espace Montmartre, page 73

All other photos: © Phil Shipman

MOON METRO PARIS
THIRD EDITION

Avalon Travel Publishing
An Imprint of Avalon Publishing Group, Inc.

Text and maps © 2006 by Avalon Travel Publishing
All rights reserved.

Paris Metro map © 2005 La Régie Autonome des Transports Parisens
(RATP). Used with permission.

Some photos and illustrations are used by permission and are the property of the original copyright owners.

ISBN-10: 1-56691-940-1
ISBN-13: 978-1-56691-940-1
ISSN: 1539-1000

Editors: Grace Fujimoto, Chris Jones
Series Manager: Grace Fujimoto
Design: Jacob Goolkasian
Map Design: Mike Morgenfeld
Production Coordinator: Jacob Goolkasian
Graphics Coordinator: Stefano Boni
Cartographer: Suzanne Service
Map Editor: Kat Smith
Fact Checkers: Belinda Aucott, Cordelia Carvonis, Stephen Heyman
Front cover photos: Eiffel Tower and Place de la Concorde, Paris,
France , © photolibrary. All rights reserved. / Sign for Metro Transit
Station in Paris, © Royalty-Free/Corbis
Printed in China through Colorcraft Ltd., Hong Kong
Printing History
1st edition – 2002
3rd edition – May 2006
5 4 3 2 1

Please send all feedback about this book to:

Moon Metro Paris
Avalon Travel Publishing
1400 65th Street, Suite 250
Emeryville, CA 94608, USA
email: feedback@moon.com
website: www.moon.com

Covering eighteen major cities throughout the world, MOON METRO takes travel to a new level with its innovative fusion of discreet maps and insider advice.

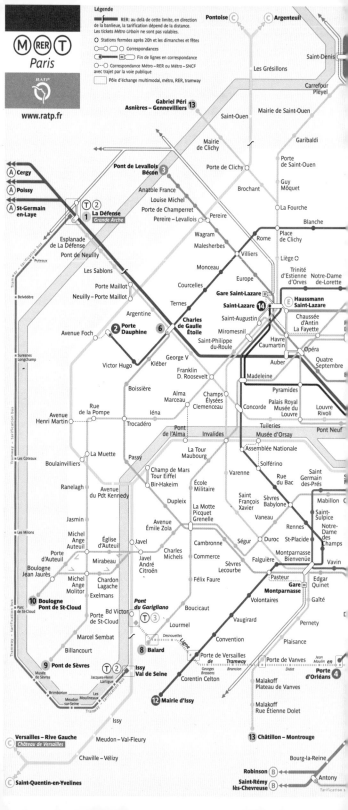